The Qurʾānic Term *Kalāla*

Journal of Arabic and Islamic Studies Monograph Series 1

The Qur'ānic Term *Kalāla*

Studies in Arabic Language and Poetry, *Ḥadīṯ*, *Tafsīr*, and *Fiqh*

Notes on the Origins of Islamic Law

Agostino Cilardo

Edinburgh University Press

Edinburgh University Press Ltd
22 George Square, Edinburgh

Transferred to Digital Printing 2007

Printed and bound in Great Britain by
CPI Antony Rowe, Eastbourne

A CIP record for this book is available from the British Library

ISBN-10 0 7486 1916 X (hardback)
ISBN-13 978 0 7486 1916 0 (hardback)

The publisher acknowledges a subsidy from the Università degli Studi di Napoli 'L'Orientale' and the Instituto Italiano per l'Africa e l'Oriente (Rome)

JAIS MONOGRAPHS
SERIES EDITOR: JOSEPH NORMENT BELL

THE QUR'ĀNIC TERM *KALĀLA*

Studies in Arabic Language and Poetry, *Ḥadīṯ*, *Tafsīr*, and *Fiqh*
Notes on the Origins of Islamic Law

Agostino Cilardo

The term *kalāla* (meaning leaving no parents or children as heirs) occurs twice in the Qur'ān. Wide divergences exist regarding its interpretation both in translations of the Qur'ān and amongst scholars, while dictionaries generally pass over its technical meaning.

This book discusses the origins of these diverging views regarding collateral inheritance, drawing on early poetry, the works of lexicographers and grammarians, *Ḥadīṯ*, Qur'ānic commentary, and numerous works of jurisprudence. It demonstrates how the particular interpretation of the term *kalāla* by the law schools enabled jurists to create new rules in areas of inheritance law that were not covered by Qur'ānic provisions and which may not correspond to the original intention of Muḥammad.

Agostino Cilardo is Professor of Islamic Law at the Università degli Studi di Napoli 'L'Orientale', Naples.

CONTENTS

ACKNOWLEDGMENTS

I wish to express my gratitude to Prof. W. Heinrichs (Harvard University), to Prof. W. B. Hallaq (McGill University), and to Prof. F. Vogel (Harvard Law School), who read my work with great care and offered many useful suggestions. Likewise I am indebted to Prof. Joseph N. Bell (University of Bergen), who went through the final draft of this study in depth and made further valuable suggestions. Finally, I would like to thank the Università degli Studi di Napoli "L'Orientale" (Naples) and the Istituto Italiano per l'Africa e l'Oriente (Rome) for providing the financial support for the publication of the work.

INTRODUCTION

The term *kalāla* occurs twice in the Qur'ān, *Sūra* 4:12 ("... If the man or woman whose inheritance is in question, *has left neither ascendants nor descendants* [*kalālat^{an}*], but has left a brother or a sister, ...") and *Sūra* 4:176 ("They ask thee for a legal decision. Say: God directs (thus) about *those who leave no descendants or ascendants as heirs* [*fī 'l-kalālat^{i}*] ...").[1] Wide divergences exist concerning its interpretation both in translations of the Qur'ān and among Western scholars, while the dictionaries generally pass over its technical meaning.[2] However, Arabic

---

[1] Cf. *The Holy Qur'ān,* text, translation, and commentary by A. Yūsuf ʿAlī (Lahore, 1938). Italics and additions in brackets mine.

[2] See my "Preliminary Notes on the Qur'ānic Term *Kalāla,*" in *Law, Christianity and Modernism in Islamic Society: Proceedings of the Eighteenth Congress of the Union Européenne des Arabisants et Islamisants, Held at the Katholieke Universiteit Leuven (September 3 – September 9, 1996)* (Louvain 1998), 3–12. The question of the interpretation of the word *kalāla* has been treated by D. S. Powers in the context of his theory on the formation of the Islamic law of inheritance (*Studies in Qur'an and* Ḥadīth: *The Formation of the Islamic Law of Inheritance* [Berkeley, Los Angeles, and London 1986]). However, his historical reconstruction has been the object of criticism by Western scholars. I myself have reviewed Powers's book, making some critical observations (see "Lo sviluppo del diritto ereditario islamico, secondo David S. Powers," in my *Teorie sulle origini del diritto islamico* [Rome 1990], 157–94; and my "Preliminary Notes"). B. G. Weiss (*MESA Bulletin* 21 [1987]: 247–48) believes that the book of Powers has much to offer; however, he states that it goes too far in claiming to give a revisionist account of the formation of Islamic law. H. Motzki (*Der Islam* 65 [1988]: 117–20) does not follow Powers in central points. Motzki's basic reservation is that Powers seems to treat the traditions of the Prophet and of the *ṣaḥāba* as historical sources. Hence Motzki draws a series of assertions and conclusions that he submits to strict criticism. However, Motzki finds that Powers's reconstruction of a proto-Islamic intestate law of inheritance is convincing. A. Rippin (*Bulletin of the School of Oriental and African Studies* 51 [1988]: 323–24) believes that "Powers's treatment of how the exegetical tradition has dealt with the various verses ... is quite masterful and provides an excellent introduction to such material in general"; Rippin states, however, that he "can hardly agree with the way Powers has pursued the question in historical terms." In particular, "crucial is the attitude taken towards the historical authenticity of the material with which he is dealing." Some reports are treated by Powers as historical accounts, "while Powers is willing to admit that the details of the actual substance of *ḥadīṯ* material might be ques-

linguistic as well as traditionist and juridical sources do stress the questions arising from the interpretation of these two Qurʾānic verses. In brief, these are: 1) There are divergences in the reading of Qurʾān 4:12; 2) Who is meant by *kalāla*? 3) Which is the word governing the accusative case of *kalāla*? and 4) What is the proper exegesis of the word *kalāla*? On the margin of these main issues, there are two other items that are also essential: 1) Was Qurʾān 4:176 the latter of the two verses revealed? and 2) Where was it revealed?

Apart from some poetic verses, the sources examined here are the most important among the linguistic, *ḥadīṯ,* and juridical works. However, not all of them treat this issue explicitly, and their authors do not seem to posit any problem.

In this monograph, a part of my investigation into the origins of the institution of the Islamic law of inheritance,[3] I attempt to shed light upon

---

tionable." Moreover, Rippin notes a lack of any discussion of what the Ǧaʿfarī school's position is on the law of inheritance. Lastly, F. J. Ziadeh (*Journal of the American Oriental Society* 108 [1988]: 487–88) differs basically with the central thesis of Powers; that is, his impossible rereading and reinterpretation of Qurʾān 4:12. The fact that the first generation of Muslims would deliberately alter the Qurʾānic text is a serious and improbable charge. And the reconstruction suggested by the author to arrive at the "original" text is impossible linguistically and semantically.

[3] See my *Teorie sulle origini del diritto islamico* (Rome 1990); *Diritto ereditario islamico delle scuole giuridiche ismailita e imamita: Casistica* (Rome and Naples 1993); *Diritto ereditario islamico delle scuole giuridiche sunnite (ḥanafita, mālikita, šāfiʿīta e ḥanbalita) e delle scuole giuridiche zaydita, ẓāhirita e ibāḍita: Casistica* (Rome and Naples 1994); "Ricerche sul lessico arabo, terminologia giuridica: Termini relativi al diritto successorio in Egitto," *AIUON* 39 (1979): 7–44; "Un antico documento di diritto ereditario musulmano," *AIUON* 42 (1982): 103–26; "La rappresentazione nel diritto ereditario musulmano," in *Atti del Congresso Internazionale su: Gli interscambi culturali e socio-economici fra l'Africa Settentrionale e l'Europa Mediterranea (Amalfi, 5 – 8 dicembre 1983),* 2 vols. (Naples 1986), II, 931–41; "Historical Development of the Legal Doctrine Relative to the Position of the Hermaphrodite in the Islamic Law," *The Search: Journal for Arab and Islamic Studies* 7 (1986): 128–70; "The Position of the Grandfather with Regard to the Full or Consanguine Brothers in the Islamic Law of Inheritance: A Reconsideration," *Annali I.U.O.*, Supplement no. 63 to vol. 50 (1990): 1–32; "'The Superimposition Theory' in the Islamic Law of Inheritance," 14th Congress of the U.E.A.I., Budapest, August 29 – September 3, 1988, *Annali I.U.O.,* Supplement no. 63 to vol. 50 (1990): 33–41; "The Position of the Slave in the Islamic Law of Inheritance: A Reconsideration," Conference of the School of Abbasid Studies, University of

what presumably were the rules concerning succession and related practice intended by *Sūra*s 4:12 and 4:176, and also upon the doctrinal changes that came about some time after the Prophet's death. It may well be that the juridical elaboration of the schools does not correspond to the original intention of Muḥammad.

Through the examination of a single word, *kalāla,* it is possible to throw light on doctrinal development beginning with some evidence found in Arabic poetry, the words of the Qur'ān, and traditionist reports, and subsequently on through the elaboration of each school of law. This research might be a contribution to the debate among Western scholars about the origins of Islamic jurisprudence and the related question of the foreign influence on Islamic law. Juynboll[4] and Motzki[5] have recently stressed the question of the authenticity of the traditions, focusing on the *isnād*s in order to date them. In particular, Motzki proved the reliability of the reports regarding the *fiqh* of al-Zuhrī[6] and sketched the early development of Meccan *fiqh* with its major figures, relying mainly on the *Muṣannaf* of ᶜAbd al-Razzāq.[7] However, their investigations differ as regards both the sources they used and their criticism.[8] The approach of Juynboll and Motzki certainly presents elements of interest. But there is a tendency to examine in particular the transmitters abstractly rather than the juridical questions involved; the debate concerns the reliability of the *isnād*s *per se* with little consideration of the *matn*s. For my part, I have chosen a different method. My starting point is that the *ḥadīṯ*s were used

St. Andrews, Scotland, July 31 – August 5, 1989, *Annali I.U.O.,* Supplement no. 63 to vol. 50 (1990): 43–57; "The Transmission of the Patronate in Islamic Law," in *Proceedings of the XVth Congress of the U.E.A.I., Utrecht, September 13 – 19, 1990,* in *Miscellanea arabica et islamica: Dissertationes in Academia Ultrajectina prolatae anno MCMXC* (Louvain 1993), 31–52.

[4] G. H. A. Juynboll, "Nāfiᶜ, the *Mawlā* of Ibn ᶜUmar, and His Position in Muslim *Ḥadīth* Literature," *Der Islam* 70 (1993): 207–44. See also his works quoted there.

[5] H. Motzki, "The *Muṣannaf* of ᶜAbd al-Razzāq al-Ṣanᶜānī as a Source of Authentic *Aḥādīth* of the First Century A.H.," *Journal of Near Eastern Studies* 50 (1991): 1–21; *Die Anfänge der islamischen Jurisprudenz: Ihre Entwicklung in Mekka bis zur Mitte des 2./8. Jahrhunderts* (Stuttgart 1991), especially 50–67.

[6] H. Motzki, "Der Fiqh des -Zuhrī: die Quellenproblematik," *Der Islam* 68 (1991): 1–44.

[7] H. Motzki, *Die Anfänge.* On the different views of Juynboll and Motzki about the authenticity of the traditions regarding al-Zuhrī, see Motzki, "Der Fiqh des -Zuhrī," 2, n. 7, and Juynboll, "Nāfiᶜ, the *Mawlā* of Ibn ᶜUmar," 226, n. 28.

[8] See H. Motzki, "The *Muṣannaf,*" 9, n. 27.

in different centers as support for different doctrines based sometimes on a different interpretation of the wording of the Qur°ān. The *ḥadīṯ*s cannot be understood outside the context of the debate on the question that they refer to. The traditions offered the basic elements for doctrinal elaboration. This means that my particular concern is to collect all the traditions available on a certain subject, to trace them back to the different centers where they originated, and to compare their *matn*s to the word of the Qur°ān, to each other, and to the doctrines of the different law schools. I do not claim to date the *ḥadīṯ*s; there may be no definite method for this up to now. What I believe important is the fact that they indicate a trend in doctrinal evolution.

In the period after the death of the Prophet, new needs emerged in Islamic society. It was realized that strict application of the Qur°ānic verses on inheritance would lead to a situation of inequity for some relatives. In particular, there are two cases in which contrasting claims oppose one another. The first regards the grandfather, who is not mentioned in the Qur°ān; the second is the question of full or consanguine sisters inheriting together with daughters. If we consider the diverging solutions of these two cases given by the different law schools, we are not able to interpret exactly Qur°ān 4:12 and 4:176. It is not so much the different definitions of *kalāla* that change the content of the Qur°ānic verses, but rather the interpretations of these definitions. It is possible that the original meaning of the term in the two Qur°ānic verses was single and well known by the people in the first decades of Islam, something I shall try to discover. The examination of the implications of the term *kalāla* can be taken as a paradigm of the complex question of the formation of juridical doctrine, for we can see how the letter of the Qur°ān was adapted to demands arising from new situations.

Some years ago, Powers gave an intriguing interpretation of Qur°ān 4:12 and 4:176.[9] He carefully examined the traditions on *kalāla* found in the *tafsīr* of al-Ṭabarī. He put special stress on those *ḥadīṯ*s that "attest to a significant amount of confusion with regard to the meaning of this word in the years immediately following the death of Muḥammad,"[10] and centered on the figure of ᶜUmar. According to Powers, they could give

[9] D. S. Powers, "The Islamic Law of Inheritance Reconsidered: A New Reading of Q. 4:12b," *Studia Islamica* 55 (1982): 61–94; and *Studies in Qur'an and* Ḥadīth: *The Formation of the Islamic Law of Inheritance* (1986). See my review of Powers's book in *Teorie,* 157–94.

[10] "The Islamic law .of Inheritance," 71.

an alternative explanation of the meaning of Qurʾān 4:12 and 4:176: "They were put into circulation by persons who clearly objected to the traditional interpretation, and who themselves viewed the two verses in an entirely different light."[11] Besides several other original proposals, Powers suggests the theory that *kalāla* "was originally a loan word from one of the four above-mentioned Semitic languages" (Akkadian, Aramaic, Syriac, and Hebrew),[12] meaning a feminine kinship term "whose semantic value embraced one or more of the concepts 'bride,' 'daughter-in-law,' and 'sister-in-law.'"[13] He maintains that after the Prophet's death the reading of Qurʾān 4:12 was manipulated, and the system elaborated by Muḥammad consequently undermined. In particular, the possibility of designating an heir was eliminated. My work may verify these assumptions. The traditions related by al-Ṭabarī, however, could be interpreted in a different way if we consider them in a wider context, that is, in closer connection with the debate on a number of juridical questions. Perhaps it is not necessary to suppose a foreign derivation of the term *kalāla.*

October 1997

[11] Ibid., 73.
[12] Ibid., 82.
[13] Ibid., 83.

CHAPTER ONE

POETRY: *KALĀLA* AS COLLATERALS

Certain verses containing the word *kalāla* are of extreme importance in seeking the original meaning of this term, both because some of them go back to the *Ǧāhiliyya* period or to the very beginning of Islam, to the same time when the Qurʾān was revealed, and because none have religious relevance. Consequently these texts offer the double advantage of reflecting untainted Arabic language and avoiding the doctrinal problems arising from the interpretation of the Qurʾān.

An Anonymous Poet

An anonymous poet proclaimed:[1]

فإن أبـا المرء أحمـى لـه   ومولى الكلالة لا يغضب

Surely, a father protects more wrathfully his offspring,
while a patron of collaterals does not get angry.

According to al-Azharī's gloss,[2] this statement demonstrates that the father does not belong to the *kalāla,*[3] while the remaining agnates (*sāʾir al-awliyāʾ min al-ʿaṣaba*), aside from *walad,* are *kalāla.* Further, this verse means that a father is more angry on behalf of his offspring, when they are unjustly treated, while the patrons of the *kalāla,* i.e., of the brothers, paternal uncles, paternal uncles' sons, and the remaining relatives, do not get angry in their defense as a father would.

This explanation shows clearly that *kalāla* refers to all male relatives, except *wālid* and *walad.* The word *mawlā* (pl. *mawālī*) seems to indicate a "patron," rather than a "client,"[4] because a patron, not a client, is entitled to grant protection. It is worth noting that the patron acts in the place of the agnates, if they are not present, being considered the last in the list of the agnates. In this respect, the interpretation of D. S. Powers does not correspond to the sense of the above verse when he writes: "Now, according to the principle of *ʿaṣabiyya* (group feeling) analyzed so brilliantly by Ibn Ḫaldūn, one can expect as much support from a brother as

---

[1] *Tahḏīb luġa,* IX, 448. It is repeated in *Aḥkām Qurʾān,* I, 448; *Lisān,* XI, 593; *Tafsīr Ṭūsī,* III, 136; *Tāǧ,* VIII, 101.

[2] *Tahḏīb luġa,* IX, 448. It is repeated in *Lisān,* XI, 593, and *Tāǧ,* VIII, 101.

[3] On this doctrine see also *Tafsīr Ṭūsī,* III, 136.

[4] as Powers (Powers, 41) has translated.

from a father."[5] Nor can we solve this difficulty "if we assume that the word *kalāla* was used in this verse in the sense of a female in-law, in which case the verse would indicate that one can expect greater support from one's father and, by extension, from one's blood relatives, than from the clients of an in-law,"[6] because this does not correspond to the intent of the anonymous poet.

However, al-Saraḫsī[7] reports this verse in a rather different way, which, nevertheless, does not change the meaning of the term *kalāla:*

وإن اب المرء حمالة   ومولى الكلالة لا يعصب

Surely, a father is a support for his offspring,
while a patron of collaterals does not surround [them].

Why is there such a difference between the two readings? And why was this verse always related anonymously, while for the other verses the name of the poets is always cited? Was it created for this particular context, or was it a product of popular wisdom?

Al-A^cšā Maymūn b. Qays

A verse by an ancient Arab poet, al-A[c]šā Maymūn b. Qays[8] (d. about 8/629), in which the word *kalāla* appears, shows that the original meaning of *kalāla* is the falling away of vigor. Despite the existence of some variations in the verse concerned, it is evident that the term is used in this context in its common meaning.

Although the verse we are concerned with is not found in the *Dīwān*[9] of al-A[c]šā, it is part of a panegyric devoted to Muḥammad ascribed to him that comprises twenty-four verses.[10] In verses 12 and 13 we find:

وآليت لا أرثِى لها من كلالة   ولا من حفا حتى تزور محمدا
متى ما تناخِى عند باب ابن هاشم   تريحِى وتلقى من فواضله يدا

This panegyric is repeated in the *Sīra* by Ibn Isḥāq,[11] but with some

[5] Ibid., 41–42.
[6] Ibid., 42.
[7] *Mabsūṭ,* XXIX, 153.
[8] Al-A[c]šā was a Christian educated at Ḥīra, who traveled much and whose main activity was writing panegyrics. It is doubtful whether he converted to Islam. *EI*[2], I, 689–90; *GAS,* II, 130–32; *GAL,* I, 31, no. 2; S, I, 65–67, no. 2; Weil, 49–50.
[9] Cf. *Dīwān A[c]šā.*
[10] *A[c]šā,* 243–60.
[11] *Sīra,* I, 255–56.

variations in the text, and with verses 10/11 and 21/24 being exchanged:

وآليت لا آوي لهـا مـن كِلالـة ولا من حفـا حتـي تلاقي محمدا
متي ما تناخي عند باب ابن هاشم تـراحـي وتلقي من فـواضلـه ندا

The *Sīra* was translated into English by Guillaume; however, the text of the panegyric was omitted there. Weil,[12] on the other hand, included it in his translation:

> Ich habe geschworen weder auf Müdigkeit
> noch auf wunde Füsse zu achten, bis es Mohammed erreicht,
> wenn es vor der Thüre des Sohnes Haschim's niederkniet,
> mag es ruhen und von dessen Güte freigebig beschenkt werden.

Lastly, the single verse 12 is quoted in *Tafsīr Nīsābūrī:*[13]

فا آلـيت لا أرثـى لها مـن كلالـة ولا من وحـى حتى تلاقى محمدا

ᶜĀmir b. al-Ṭufayl

Another verse containing the term *kalāla* was composed by ᶜĀmir b. al-Ṭufayl[14] (d. 10/632), who belonged to the tribe of the ᶜĀmir b. Ṣaᶜṣaᶜa. He was born in 570 A.D., and after his father's death he became the *šayḫ* of the Ǧaᶜfar b. Kilāb. He took part in many battles against the neighboring tribes. In the year 9 or 10, he paid a visit to the Prophet, but he did not become a Muslim. Shortly after, he died at the age of about 62. He wrote some 50 poems, the theme of most of them being *faḫr* and *hiğāʾ*, but seldom in the form of a *qaṣīda.* They are a true reflection of the atmosphere of his time and the nature of its poetry.[15]

The *Dīwān* by Ibn al-Ṭufayl has been edited and translated by Lyall.[16] In one place the Arabic text of this verse is at pp. 92–93 (Arabic portion) and the English translation at p. 95 (English portion), the second of three very celebrated and often cited verses. It is written in the commonest of the Arabic meters, *ṭawīl.*[17] However, the word *kalāla* is not used here, but rather *qarāba:*

إنـي وإن كنـت ابن سـيد عـامر وفارسها المندوب في كل موكب
فمـا سودتنى عـامر عن قرابة أبـى الله أن أسمـو بـأم ولا أب

---

[12] *Leben Mohammed,* I, 190–91.

[13] IV, 201.

[14] *Aᶜlām,* IV, 20; *Dīwāns,* 73–93; *EI,* I, 330; *EI²*, I, 442; *GAL,* S, I, 57–58, no. 15; *GAS,* II, 244–45; *Littérature,* 79–80.

[15] *GAS,* II, 245.

[16] Cf. *Dīwāns.*

[17] On this meter, see *EI,* VIII, 704; *Dīwāns,* translations XLVIII–L.

ولكننـى أحمـى حمـاهـا وأتقـى   أذاهـا وأرمى من رمـاها بمنكب

As for me, though I be the son of the Chief of ᶜĀmir,
and the Knight of the tribe, called on for help in every adventure,
It was not for my kinsmen's sake that ᶜĀmir made me their chief:
God forbid that I should exalt myself on mother's or father's fame!
But it was because I guard their peculiar land, and shield them from annoy,
and hurl myself against him that strikes at their peace.

In another place, these verses are the last three of a poem of ten verses. The complete text is cited in the *Supplement* to the same work of Lyall, at pp. 152–53 (Arabic portion, no. 1), and at pp. 120–21 (English portion, no. 1). Now, the *Supplement*[18] has *wirāṯa* instead of *qarāba*, as it is in the *Kitāb al-Šiᶜr waʾl-šuᶜarāʾ*[19] of Ibn Qutayba[20] (d. 276/889). The philologist Ibn Rašīq[21] (d. 456/1064), in his *Kitāb al-ᶜUmda,*[22] also has *wirāṯa.* Further, the Arabic text in the two places in Lyall does not correspond perfectly, and consequently his translation is not the same. Concerning the verse in question, the *Supplement*[23] has:

Yet ᶜĀmir has not made me its Lord because I inherited the place
God forbid that I should rise upon mother's or father's fame!

It is clear that this variant reading *wirāṯa* is completely outside our field, but the variant *qarāba,* at least generically, refers to kinship, thus constituting some justification for the use of this verse in the context of *kalāla.* Only later sources, like *Lisān al-ᶜArab, Maǧmaᶜ, Tafsīr al-Ṭusī,* and *Tāǧ al-ᶜarūs,* cite *kalāla;*[24] and this reading was found in a book by al-Rāzī quoted by al-Ṭusī without naming the work:[25]

وما سودتـني عـامر عن كلالة   أبى الله أن أسمـو بـأم ولا أب

It was not for my collateral kinsmen's sake that ᶜĀmir made me their chief:
God forbid that I should exalt myself on mother's or father's fame!

I believe that *kalāla* should be translated as "collateral kinsmen" in

---

[18] Cf. Arabic portion, p. 153. Also in *Maǧmaᶜ,* II, 17; *Tafsīr Ṭūsī,* III, 136.

[19] Cf. *Poësis,* 192.

[20] *GAL,* I, 124–27, no. 1; S, I, 184–87, no. 1; *GAS,* III, 376–77; IV, 344; VII, 350–51; VIII, 161–65; IX, 154–58.

[21] *GAL,* I, 374, no. 1; S, I, 539–40, no. 1; *GAS,* IX, 263.

[22] *ᶜUmda Ibn Rašīq,* II, 146.

[23] English portion, p. 121.

[24] *Dīwāns,* 92, n. 1; *Lisān,* XI, 593; *Maǧmaᶜ,* II, 16–17; *Tafsīr Ṭūsī,* III, 136; *Tāǧ,* VIII, 102. *Tafsīr Ṭūsī,* and *Maǧmaᶜ* have فما .

[25] *Tafsīr Ṭūsī,* III, 136.

this context because this is the Šīᶜī interpretation reported by the Šīᶜīs al-Ṭusī and al-Ṭabarsī (*Maǧmaᶜ*), and by the Sunnī al-Rāzī as well, and repeated, presumably, in *Lisān al-ᶜArab* and *Tāǧ al-ᶜarūs.* One may wonder why the most ancient dictionaries do not contain this verse and why this change was made. Was it a clumsy attempt to give support to an interpretation of the term *kalāla?*

Ziyāda b. Zayd al-ᶜUḏrī

Two Imāmī sources, *Tafsīr Ṭusī*[26] and *Maǧmaᶜ*,[27] relate a verse containing the word *kalāla* by the poet Ziyāda b. Zayd al-ᶜUḏrī,[28] who lived in the Ḥiǧāz during the last years of the *Ǧāhiliyya* and the early Islamic period. He was killed about 54/674 by his brother-in-law and rival, Hudba b. al-Ḫašram.[29] Even if we presume that the verse by ᶜĀmir b. al-Ṭufayl discussed above was subsequently altered, the line by Ziyāda provides an ancient example of the use of the term *kalāla* in a poem:

ولم أرث المجد التليد كلالة　　　ولم يـأن منـي فترة لعقيب

I did not inherit ancestral glory as a collateral,
and the time has not come for me to yield to a successor.

The use of the term *kalāla* in this context suggests that we are in presence of glory, nobility, or honor, transmitted from father to sons in a direct patrilinear line, not through collaterals. This interpretation is supported by the words *al-maǧd al-talīd* (ancestral glory), which refer to the ancestors of one's own family or tribe. Moreover, in *Maǧmaᶜ*,[30] it is said that a variant reading has *qarīb* instead of *ᶜaqīb.* Now the term *qarīb* better expresses that this *al-maǧd al-talīd* passes on to a close relative, viz., to one's son.

Al-Farazdaq Hammām b. Ġālib

A verse by the poet al-Farazdaq Hammām[31] b. Ġālib[32] (d. 110/728) is reported in many sources, but with some variant readings, which, however, do not distort its meaning. Al-Farazdaq, the famous Arab satirist and panegyrist, was born at the end of the caliphate of ᶜUmar in about

---

[26] III, 136. There the name is "Ziyād" rather than "Ziyāda."

[27] II, 17. There the *nisba* is الغدري instead of العذري.

[28] *GAS,* II, 266; *Tables,* II, 362.

[29] Ibid., 265.

[30] II, 17, n. 1.

[31] *EI²,* II, 788, has "Tammām."

[32] *Aᶜlām,* IX, 96–97; *EI,* III, 60–61; *EI²,* II, 788–89; *GAL,* I, 49–52; S, I, 84–85; *GAS,* II, 359–63; *Littérature,* 121–29.

the year 20/641. He was representative of a generation torn between Bedouin culture and the new ethics. He belonged to *ahl al-Baṣra,* and he had a vast knowledge of the Arabic language. In this regard it is said: "If it were not for al-Farazdaq's poetry, one-third of the language of the Arabs and one-half of the traditions of the people would have been lost."[33] He died at Baṣra in about the year 110/728.

The verse by al-Farazdaq, concerning the Banū Umayya, is inserted in a poem written on the death of Qutayba b. Muslim al-Bāhilī (d. 96/714–15) who was killed by Wakīᶜ b. Ḥassān.[34] The Arabic text is quoted in *Šarḥ Dīwān al-Farazdaq*[35] and in *Dīwān al-Farazdaq,*[36] but it is not found in Boucher[37] and Hell.[38]

Taking as a basis the text of al-Ǧawharī (d. 393/1003), *Tāǧ al-luġa,*[39] it is:

ورثتم قنـــاة الملك غـير كلالـــة عن ابني مناف عبد شمس وهاشم

You inherited the scepter of kingship, not as collaterals,
from the sons of Manāf, ᶜAbd Šams and Hāšim.[40]

Ibn Manẓūr's gloss[41] is that "you inherited it as a close relationship (*qurb*), not as a remote one (*buᶜd*)." Hence, the transmission of the power passes through a direct line, not through a collateral line.

In some sources there is *lā ᶜan* instead of *ġayr.*[42] This leads to a small change in the meaning of the verse, but it does not alter the sense of the

---

[33] *Aᶜlām,* IX, 96.

[34] Cf. *Divan Farazdak,* 22; *Divan Férazdak,* 136, n. 1.

[35] p. 852, verse no. 30. The poem consists of 159 verses.

[36] II, 309, verse no. 30. Here the poem consists of 149 verses, because verses no. 95–100 and 156–59 of the previous text are omitted.

[37] *Divan Férazdak.*

[38] *Divan Farazdak.*

[39] II, 592; it is repeated in *Lisān,* XI, 592, and in *Tāǧ,* VIII, 101. *Aḥkām Qurᵓān* (I, 448), *Mabsūṭ* (XXIX, 153), and *Muġnī* (VII, 5) have *al-maǧd* instead of *al-mulk. Ḫilāf* (II, 264), *Dīwān al-Farazdaq* (II, 309), and *Šarḥ Dīwān al-Farazdaq* (p. 852), have *ibn* instead of *ibnay.* However, later on *Dīwān al-Farazdaq* (II, 316, verse 2) and *Šarḥ Dīwān al-Farazdaq* (p. 859, verse 11), have *ibnay Manāf.*

[40] Great-grandfather of the prophet Muḥammad. His brothers were Nawfal and ᶜAbd Šams. *EI²*, III, 260.

[41] *Lisān,* XI, 593. It is repeated in *Tāǧ,* VIII, 102.

[42] *Aḥkām Qurᵓān,* I, 448; *Ḫilāf,* II, 264; *Lisān,* XI, 593; *Mabsūṭ,* XXIX, 153; *Muġnī,* VII, 5; *Tafsīr Nīsābūrī,* IV, 201; *Tafsīr Rāzī,* II, 279; *Tāǧ,* VIII, 102.

term *kalāla:* "You inherited the scepter of kingship, not from collaterals." Al-Rāzī's gloss[43] is that :

دل هذا البيت على انهم ما ورثوا الملك عن الكلالة ودل انهم ورثوها عن آبائهم وهذا يوجب أن لا يكون الاب داخلا في الكلالة ،

that is, you did not inherit the power from collaterals, but from their ancestors; thus, *ab* is never included in the concept of *kalāla.* Lastly, Ibn Qudāma[44] gives this explanation:

انكم ورثتم الملك عن آبائكم لا عن أمهاتكم ،

that is, you inherited the kingship from your paternal ancestors, not your maternal ascendants.

Powers argues, quite correctly, that "this verse is often cited in support of the assertion that the word *kalāla* means 'all those except parent and child,'" on the basis of the gloss by Ibn Manẓūr.[45] However, we have no evidence to affirm, as Powers does, that "kingship may be inherited from any member of the family, including brothers, cousins, and uncles."[46] On the contrary, kingship may pass only through the male line, as one can also deduce from the verse by al-Farazdaq. Therefore, it seems unfounded that "the assumption that the word *kalāla* originally signified a female in-law may bring us closer to the meaning of this verse of poetry. It is not the degree of kinship that is at issue, but the very fact of kinship. A dynasty collapses when someone who is not a member of the ruling family assumes power."[47]

Qays b. Ḏarīḥ

Kitāb al-Aġānī[48] has a long passage regarding the love affair between Qays b. Ḏarīḥ and Lubnā bint Ḥubāb al-Kaᶜbiyya, where the word *kalāla* occurs. Powers has examined and translated this passage.[49] In brief, "Qays fell in love with Lubnā and married her against the wishes of his parents, who wanted him to marry one of his paternal cousins. Qays's mother became jealous of Lubnā, claiming that Qays had become more responsive to his wife than to his mother. After Qays recovered from a

[43] *Tafsīr Rāzī,* II, 379.

[44] *Muġnī,* VII, 5.

[45] Powers, 41.

[46] Ibid.

[47] Ibid.

[48] VIII, 111–34.

[49] Powers, 41–42, n. 36. The translation of the text is in appendix B, pp. 219–22.

near-fatal illness, his mother seized upon Lubnā's barrenness as a pretext to get rid of the woman, saying to her husband, 'I was afraid that Qays would die without leaving descendants, for that woman [viz., Lubnā] is barren. You are a wealthy man, so that [if Qays had died] your property would have passed to *al-kalāla*. Therefore, marry him to another woman—perhaps God will provide him with children.'"[50]

Powers infers that "the context here requires that *'kalāla'* refer to Lubnā, Umm Qays's *daughter-in-law.*" Further, Powers argues, "*'kalāla'* here cannot refer to 'one who dies leaving neither parent nor child,' the preferred meaning of the term among Muslim lexicographers, because then the sentence becomes tautological. And it is unlikely that *'kalāla'* signifies 'all those except the parent and child,' i.e., cousins, etc., because Qays's parents had originally tried to get him to marry one of his cousins."[51]

On the contrary, I believe that *kalāla* refers here to collaterals.[52] Qays is Ḏarīḥ's only son, and his father worried that, in case of his son's death, his property would pass to collaterals instead of remaining inside his family attributed to his male descendants. For this reason, Qays suggests his father "marry [another woman], so that God might provide you with another son besides me."[53]

From the material examined above, in which the term *kalāla* occurs, I deduce that its ordinary Arabic meaning is loss of vigor, as clearly appears from the verse of al-Aᶜšā. The remaining texts support the meaning of *kalāla* as collaterals. Admittedly one cannot comment on the date and the authenticity of the verse by the anonymous poet. Moreover, as far as the verse by ᶜĀmir b. al-Ṭufayl is concerned, the variant reading undoubtedly refers to collaterals; but it can not be taken as proof of the real meaning of *kalāla,* because this reading can be found only in later sources that might have adapted the verse to their particular interpretation. In fact, some sources (al-Ṭusī, al-Ṭabarsī, al-Rāzī) refer to the Imāmī and Ismāᶜīlī doctrine that *kalāla* are collaterals, while some others (*Lisān al-ᶜArab, Tāǧ al-ᶜarūs*) may have uncritically reported this variant. On the other hand, no doubt can arise concerning the attribution of the verses by Ziyāda and al-Farazdaq, or about the literary authenticity of the report in

[50] Ibid., 41, n. 36.

[51] Ibid., 41–42, n. 36.

[52] H. Motzki (*Der Islam* 65 [1988]: 118) and F. J. Ziadeh (*Journal of the American Oriental Society* 108 [1988]: 488) interpret the passage similarly.

[53] Translation, Powers, 222.

the *Kitāb al-Aġānī* regarding the love affair between Qays and Lubnā. Thus, according to the most ancient and non-religious sources, *kalāla* refers to collateral kinsmen. In short, while the usual sense of the word *kalāla* is feebleness, it means collaterals with reference to kinship.

CHAPTER TWO

LINGUISTIC ELABORATION

The linguists are aware of the doctrinal implication of the term *kalāla:* they are to some extent interested in the questions involved and do not shy away from explaining the *tafsīr, ḥadīṯ,* and *fiqh* literatures. For instance, the disciple of al-Kisāʾī, the Kūfan scholar al-Liḥyānī,[1] reflects the correct juridical rule when he says that *kalāla* are those *ᶜaṣaba* with whom uterine siblings can inherit,[2] thus referring the term to siblings and to all remaining *ᶜaṣaba* (except *walad,* offspring, and *wālid,* parent) who do not exclude uterine siblings. This view is significant because Liḥyānī's *Kitāb al-Nawādir* was among the major sources for Ibn Sīda's (d. 458/1066) *Kitāb al-Muḥkam,* and many quotations from it can be found in the *Tahḏīb al-luġa,* in the *Lisān al-ᶜArab,* and other lexicographical works. Moreover, there is an anonymous statement[3] to the effect that *kalāla* are the uterine siblings, which undoubtedly refers to a juridical question. In sum, the linguistic sources are very important because they make explicit the two meanings of the term *kalāla* found in the poetic sources; in fact, they give two different definitions of it based on those meanings, proving them through different etymologies.

SOURCES

Sezgin has given a comprehensive account of the beginnings, the rise, and the development of Arabic lexicography.[4] The sources used here offer a view of the whole lexicographical tradition elaborated by the Arabs. They reflect the doctrine of the various geographical areas where a debate on the Arabic language developed.

The most ancient source available is the *Kitāb al-ᶜAyn* by al-Ḫalīl b. Aḥmad al-Baṣrī[5] (d. 175/791). This work is not arranged alphabetically,

---

[1] *GAS,* VIII, 126, 271; *Iršād,* V, 299–300; *Tāǧ,* I, 11.

[2] *Lisān,* XI, 592; *Muḥkam,* VI, 410; *Qāmūs,* IV, 45; *Tāǧ,* VIII, 101.

[3] *Ǧamhara,* I, 120; *Lisān,* XI, 592; *Muḥkam,* VI, 410; *Qāmūs,* IV, 45; *Tāǧ,* VIII, 101.

[4] *GAS,* VIII, 7–15.

[5] *EI²,* IV, 962–64; *GAL,* I, 98–99. no. 4; S, I, 159–60, no. 4; *GAS,* VIII, 51–56; IX, 44–48. There was a close relationship between al-Ḫalīl and al-Layṯ b. al-Muẓaffar (d. 190/805), the *ṣāḥib al-Ḫalīl,* an Arab philologist and jurisprudent, who revised, completed, edited, and published al-Ḫalīl's lexicon. We find

but rather according to the phonetic-permutative system. Ḫalīl was the first to attempt to compile a comprehensive Arabic lexicon on the basis of several previous works, claiming to have collected the whole Arabic lexical repertoire. For this reason, his authorship of this work was rejected by most scholars.

Ibn Durayd[6] (d. 321/933), a preeminent representative of the Baṣran school, wrote a monumental dictionary, *al-Ǧamhara fī ʾl-luġa,* his chief work. He made use of the *Kitāb al-ʿAyn* by Ḫalīl, but selecting and arranging the words according to his own judgment. With reference to *kalāla,* he provides scanty explanation in this work and does not distinguish between strict linguistic questions and doctrinal implications.

Another important source is the *Tahḏīb al-luġa* by the Arab lexicographer al-Azharī al-Harawī[7] (d. 370/980). It is in reality a work by his master, the lexicographer al-Munḏirī al-Harawī[8] (d. 329/940). Al-Azharī wrote his *Tahḏīb al-luġa* according to the *riwāya* of al-Munḏirī, and he frequently cites him in the *Tahḏīb.* Al-Azharī had the opportunity to become particularly adept in the Arabic language, studying it with the Bedouin tribes to whom he fell prisoner. During this period he composed most of the *Tahḏīb,* a dictionary arranged according to phonetic classification, beginning with the "gutturals" and finishing with the "labials," as al-Ḫalīl had done in *Kitāb al-ʿAyn.* Based on the works of his master al-Munḏirī and on several additional sources, partly cited in a historical-systematical introduction, it is considered one of the greatest lexicographical works of its time.

The Arabic lexicographer of Turkish origin al-Ǧawharī[9] (d. 393/1003), wrote a widely used Arabic dictionary entitled *Tāǧ al-luġa wa-ṣiḥāḥ al-ʿarabiyya.* Although it was intended to contain only authentic lexicographical data, numerous errors can be detected in it. Al-Ǧawharī arranged the roots under the last radical, and this system was later fol-

conflicting traditions to what extent the *Kitāb al-ʿAyn* was written by al-Ḫalīl and to what extent it was edited by al-Layṯ. Many scholars solved this difficulty by using the formula *qāla ṣāḥib al-ʿAyn.*

6 *EI²,* III, 757–58; *GAL,* I, 112–14, no. 24; S, I, 172–74, no. 25, *GAS,* VIII, 101–5; IX, 85–86.

7 *Aʿlām,* VI, 202; *EI²,* I, 822; *GAL,* I, 134–35, no. 4; S, I, 197, no. 4; *GAS,* VIII, 201–5; *Iršād,* VI, 297–99.

8 *Tahḏīb luġa* (IX, 447) has: المنذِر. *Aʿlām,* VI, 298; *GAL,* I, 129, no. 6; S, I, 189, no. 6; *GAS,* VIII, 194–95; *Iršād,* VI, 464–66.

9 *EI²,* II, 495–97; *GAL,* I, 133–34, no. 3; S, I, 196–97, no. 3; *GAS,* VIII, 215–24; IX, 317.

lowed by Ibn Manẓūr (see below). The dictionary was allegedly written by him up to the letter *ḍād* and then completed by his pupil Abū Isḥāq Ibrāhīm b. Ṣāliḥ al-Warrāq. "The *Ṣiḥāḥ* contains mainly an abstract from earlier lexicographical works . . . , while al-Ǧawharī's own contributions are minimal."[10] As far as the term *kalāla* is concerned, his contribution is modest, as he is very concise; his work consists of only two volumes in the Būlāq edition.

Ibn Sīda[11] (d. 458/1066), the Andalusian philologist and lexicographer, among his many works wrote two dictionaries: the *Kitāb al-Muḥkam wa᾽l-muḥīṭ al-aᶜẓam,* which contains a short synthesis of the issues regarding *kalāla,* and the *Kitāb al-Muḫaṣṣaṣ fī ᾽l-luġa,* a dictionary arranged according to subject. They are "dictionaries based on other dictionaries."[12]

Ibn al-Aṯīr's[13] (d. 606/1210) work examined here is his *Kitāb al-Nihāya fī ġarīb al-ḥadīṯ wa᾽l-āṯār,* a dictionary of less common words and meanings occurring in the Prophetic traditions that was subsequently incorporated into the *Lisān al-ᶜArab.* He briefly discusses *kalāla.* Al-Suyūṭī (d. 911/1505), in his *al-Durr al-naṯīr,* which is a summary of *al-Nihāya,* repeats only the commonly accepted definition of *kalāla.*

Ibn Manẓūr[14] (d. 711/1311), was fond of epitomizing voluminous works by earlier authors. His *Lisān al-ᶜArab* is particularly important because it is a synthesis of the five previous major dictionaries, viz., al-Azharī's *Tahḏīb al-luġa,* copiously used,[15] *al-Ǧamhara fī ᾽l-luġa* by Ibn Durayd, *Tāǧ al-luġa wa-ṣiḥāḥ al-ᶜarabiyya* by al-Ǧawharī, the *Kitāb al-Muḥkam wa᾽l-muḥīṭ al-aᶜẓam* by Ibn Sīda, and the *Kitāb al-Nihāya fī ġarīb al-ḥadīṯ wa᾽l-āṯār* by Ibn al-Aṯīr. Ibn Manẓūr is on the whole exact in copying these works, but often omits the authorities mentioned therein, whilst al-Zabīdī, who in his *Tāǧ al-ᶜārūs* draws frequently upon the *Lisān,* often supplies the authorities omitted by Ibn Manẓūr.

Another source, of little importance however, is *al-Qāmūs al-muḥīṭ* by the philologist and lexicographer Muḥammad b. Yaᶜqūb al-Fīrūzābādī[16] (d. 817/1415). *Al-Qāmūs* "is pre-eminently a compilation of the *Muḥkam*

---

[10] *EI²,* II, 496.

[11] *EI²,* III, 940; *GAL,* I, 376, no. 1; S, I, 542, no. 1.

[12] *EI²,* III, 940.

[13] *Aᶜlām,* VI, 152; *EI²,* III, 723–24; *GAL,* I, 438–39, no. 15; S, I, 607–9, no. 15; *GAS,* VIII, 248.

[14] *EI²,* III, 864; *GAL,* II, 25, no. 3; S, II, 14–15, no. 3.

[15] See *EI²,* I, 822.

[16] *EI²,* II, 926–27; *GAL,* II, 231–34; S, II, 234–36, no. 5.

of Ibn Sīda and of the *ᶜUbāb* of al-Ṣaġānī"[17] (d. 650/1252).[18] This work has only scarce information about *kalāla.*

Lastly, *Tāǧ al-ᶜarūs min ǧawāhir al-Qāmūs* by al-Zabīdī[19] (d. 1205/ 1791) is of great importance. *Tāǧ al-ᶜarūs* is a commentary on al-Fīrūzābādī's *al-Qāmūs al-muḥīṭ.*

The consultation of the dictionaries of each period is useful to understand the doctrinal position at that time. However, the book by al-Zabīdī, and even more, the work by Ibn Manẓūr, may be considered as syntheses of the content of all previous lexicographical works. In fact, they summarize all the doctrines elaborated in the past.

LEXICOGRAPHERS AND GRAMMARIANS

Concerning the question of the definition of the term *kalāla,* we have a significant example of a debate among the various lexicography and grammar schools beginning from the second half of the first century H. onwards.[20]

SCHOOL OF KŪFA

Al-Farrāᵓ and Ṯaᶜlab: Kalāla *are relatives other than* wālid *and* walad, *namely, collaterals:*

الكلالة ما خلا الوالد و الولد .

One of the most representative figures of the so-called Kūfan school is al-Farrāᵓ al-Kūfī[21] (d. 207/822), together with al-Aḥmar, one of the most famous followers of the Kūfan al-Kisāᵓī[22] (d. 189/805). Al-Farrāᵓ accepts the definition that *kalāla* are relatives excluding *wālid* and *walad.*[23] Hence, *kalāla* are the collaterals.

Ibn al-Aᶜrābī's disciple, Abū ᵓl-ᶜAbbās Ṯaᶜlab al-Kūfī[24] (d. 291/904),

---

[17] *EI²*, II, 926–27.

[18] *GAL,* I, 443–44, no. 21; S, I, 613–15, no. 21.

[19] *GAL,* II, 231–34, 371, no. 16; S, II, 234–36, 398–99, no. 18; *GAS,* VIII, 20, no. 10.

[20] *Tafsīr Manār* (VI, 105) briefly summarizes the various statements.

[21] *Aᶜlām,* IX, 178–79; *EI²*, II, 806–8; *GAL,* I, 118, no. 3; S, I, 178–79, no. 3; *GAS,* VIII, 123–25; IX, 131–34; *Iršād,* VII, 276–78; *Tāǧ,* I, 11.

[22] *GAL,* I, 117–18, no. 2; S, I, 177–78, no. 2; *GAS,* VIII, 117; IX, 127–31.

[23] *Tahḏīb luġa,* IX, 447. It is repeated in *Lisān,* XI, 592; *Muḥkam,* VI, 410; *Šarḥ Nīl,* VIII, 299.

[24] *EI,* VIII, 735; *GAL,* I, 121–22, no. 9; S, I, 181–82, no. 9; *GAS,* VIII, 141–47; IX, 140–42.

agrees with the definition given by al-Farrāʾ,[25] with whom he stayed for some of his earlier years and whose works he studied with great enthusiasm. There was therefore a doctrinal continuity within the presumed Kūfan school, and Ṯaʿlab represents, in particular, the preservation of al-Farrāʾ's tradition.

Ibn al-Aʿrābī: Kalāla *are the remote paternal uncle's sons, namely, remote collaterals:*

الكلالة بنو العم الأباعد .

Another representative of the Kūfan school is Ibn al-Aʿrābī al-Kūfī[26] (d. 231/846), who was a philologist and a pupil of al-Kisāʾī and others. He claims to have collected many facts from the mouths of the Bedouins, and the case of *kalāla* confirms the claim. In fact, he stresses that *kalāla* are the remote paternal uncle's sons,[27] a definition which is surely on the right track, even if it is partial, since it grasps only in part the meaning of the term and ignores closer relatives, like brothers, paternal uncles, and close paternal cousins. In support of his statement, Ibn al-Aʿrābī relates that al-Aʿrābī[28] would say: "I have considerable property and only *kalāla,* whose kinship is lower, will inherit from me (*mālī kaṯīr wa-yariṯunī kalāla mutarāḫ^{in} nasabuhum*)."[29] Certainly the report from al-Aʿrābī is quite generic; but the inference made by Ibn al-Aʿrābī is not at all complete. Ibn al-Aʿrābī maintained that the most representative scholars of the Baṣran school, Abū ʿUbayda and al-Aṣmaʿī (d. 213/828), knew nothing (in the case of Abū ʿUbayda, it seems true, at least in the case of *kalāla*); however, Ibn al-Aʿrābī himself was accused of fanciful interpretations to the extent that he was charged with ignorance. This explains why he did not have a very distinguished career. Perhaps it is not without significance that his doctrine is not quoted in the *Tahḏīb al-luġa.*

---

[25] *Tahḏīb luġa,* IX, 447.

[26] *Aʿlām,* VI, 365–66; *EI^2,* III, 706–7; *GAL,* I, 119–20, no. 6; S, I, 179–80, no. 6; *GAS,* VIII, 127–29; *Iršād,* VII, 5–9; *Tāǧ,* I, 11.

[27] *Lisān,* XI, 592; *Šarḥ Nīl,* VIII, 299; *Tāǧ,* VIII, 101; *Tāǧ luġa,* II, 236.

[28] Abū ʾl-Samaydaʿ al-Aʿrābī: *GAS,* VIII, 41, 265, cited among *Frühe Lexikographen und Fuṣaḥāʾ,* probably a Bedouin learned in the Arabic language active at the time of the governorship of ʿAbd Allāh b. Ṭāhir in Nīsābūr. But *GAS* quotes two further names: Abū Laylā al-Aʿrābī (VIII, 41, 265), who belonged to the circle of ʿAbd Allāh b. Ṭāhir in Nīsābūr, and Abū ʾl-Ġayṯ al-Aʿrābī, 44, 266), who was active in the 4th/10th century.

[29] *Lisān,* XI, 592; *Tāǧ,* VIII, 101; *Tāǧ luġa,* II, 236.

SCHOOL OF BAṢRA

Al-Ḫalīl: Kalāla *is a person who has neither* wālid *nor* walad.

Al-Ḫalīl b. Aḥmad, in his *Kitāb al-ᶜAyn,*[30] does not give a definition of the term *kalāla.* However, he defines the word *kall* as "orphan," also giving it the meaning of a person who has no *walad.* Consequently, one can deduce that it is a question of a person having neither *wālid* nor *walad.*[31] Hence, *kalāla* is a person having only collateral kinship. Also al-Ǧawharī,[32] Ibn Sīda,[33] Ibn al-Aṯīr,[34] Ibn Manẓūr,[35] al-Fīrūzābādī,[36] and al-Zabīdī[37] agree on the definition of *kalāla* as a person who has neither *walad* nor *wālid. Tāǧ luġa*[38] reports a saying of the Bedouin Arabs: "He does not inherit from him as *kalāla;* viz., not by remote kinship (*ᶜurḍ*), but by close kinship (*qurb*), and by possessing a right (*istiḥqāq*)"; i.e., not as a collateral, but in a direct line.

Abū ᶜUbayda and al-Aḫfaš: Kalāla *is a person who has neither* walad, *nor* ab, *nor brother as heir:*

الكلالة كل من لم يرثه ولد أو أب أو أخ .

The position of some representatives of the school of Baṣra seems arbitrary enough. The Arab philologist Abū ᶜUbayda al-Baṣrī[39] (d. 207/822) gave explanations of the trickiest Qurᵓānic passages from the grammatical and philological point of view. It is in this context that we may view his interpretation of *kalāla* as a person who has neither *walad* nor *ab* nor a brother as heir.[40] We may wonder why "father" instead of the more comprehensive *wālid.* Moreover, there is no apparent sense in mentioning brother (what kind of brother: a full or consanguine or uter-

---

[30] *ᶜAyn,* V, 279.

[31] *Aḥkām Qurᵓān* (I, 448) attributes to him the definition: *"Al-kalāla* is a person who has neither *walad* nor *wālid."*

[32] *Tāǧ luġa,* II, 235.

[33] *Muḥkam,* VI, 410.

[34] *Nihāya,* IV, 31.

[35] *Lisān,* XI, 592.

[36] *Qāmūs,* IV, 45.

[37] *Tāǧ,* VIII, 101.

[38] II, 235.

[39] *Aᶜlām,* VIII, 191; *EI*[2], I, 158; *GAL,* I, 102–3, no. 9; S, I, 162, no. 9; *GAS,* VIII, 67–71; IX, 65–66; *Tāǧ,* I, 10–11.

[40] *Tahḏīb luġa,* IX, 447. It is repeated in *Lisān,* XI, 592. This statement is anonymously quoted in *Aḥkām Qurᵓān,* I, 448 (where there is *wālid*) and *Šarḥ Nīl,* VIII, 299.

ine brother?) together with *walad* and father. Had Abū ᶜUbayda been influenced by those definitions of *kalāla* that referred only to the paternal uncle's sons?

Considering Abū ᶜUbayda's particular doctrine, the attribution to him in a more recent source, the *Ḫilāf*[41] by the Šīᶜī jurist al-Ṭusī (d. 460/1067), of the definition of *kalāla* as parents (*wālidān*) and offspring (*mawlūdūn*) seems quite impossible. Furthermore the Iraqi definition, attributed to Abū ᶜUbayda by the Ḥanafī jurist al-Saraḫsī (d. 483/1090),[42] and repeated by Ibn al-ᶜArabī (d. 543/1148),[43] as the deceased who has died leaving neither *walad* nor *wālid* should be considered as spurious.

The definition of *kalāla* given by Abū ᶜUbayda was shared by the contemporary Baṣran scholar, al-Aḫfaš al-Awsaṭ[44] (d. 215/830).

Abū ᶜUbayd: Kalāla *are the* ᶜaṣaba, *however low.*

Other evidence drawn from the Baṣran school is related on the authority of Ibn al-Ǧarrāḥ[45] (d. 296/908). He attributes a further expansion of the definition given by the Kūfan Ibn al-Aᶜrābī to the grammarian, Qurʾānic scholar, and lawyer Abū ᶜUbayd b. Sallām al-Harawī[46] (d. 224/838):[47]

إذا لم يكن ابن العم لحّا وكان رجلا من العشيرة قالوا: هو ابن عمي الكلالةُ وابن عم كلالةٍ وابن عمي كلالة ،

i.e., if there is no cousin in the paternal line of the first degree, but only a man belonging to the clan (kinsfolk, *ᶜašīra*), he is called a remote cousin in the paternal line. According to al-Azharī,[48] this means that the *ᶜaṣaba,*

---

[41] II, 263.

[42] *Mabsūṭ,* XXIX, 153.

[43] *Aḥkām Qurʾān,* I, 448.

[44] *Tahḏīb luġa,* IX, 447. It is repeated in *Lisān,* XI, 592. On al-Aḫfaš, see *Aᶜlām,* III, 154–55; *EI²*, I, 321; *GAL,* I, 104–5, no. 12; *GAS,* VIII, 80; IX, 68–69; *Tāǧ,* I, 11.

[45] *Tahḏīb luġa* (IX, 448) has Abū ʾl-Ǧarrāḥ. *Aᶜlām,* VI, 355; *EI²*, III, 750; *GAL,* S, I, 224–25, no. 1d; *GAS,* I, 374–75, no. 10.

[46] *EI²*, I, 157; *GAL,* I, 105–7, no. 14; S, I, 166–67, no. 14; *GAS,* VIII, 81–87; 127; IX, 70–72.

[47] *Tahḏīb luġa,* IX, 448–49. It is repeated in *Aḥkām Qurʾān,* I, 448; *Lisān,* XI, 592, 593; *Muḥkam,* VI, 410; *Qāmūs,* IV, 45; *Šarḥ Nīl,* VIII, 299; *Tāǧ,* VIII, 101; *Tāǧ luġa,* II, 236.

[48] *Tahḏīb luġa,* IX, 449. It is repeated in *Lisān,* XI, 593; *Tāǧ,* VIII, 101.

however low, are designated as *kalāla*. The doctrine accepted by Abū ᶜUbayd confirms that he was an eclectic scholar following the grammatical schools of both Baṣra and Kūfa.[49]

ETYMOLOGY

Kalāla *derived from* takallala: *collaterals are* kalāla

The scholars who believe that *kalāla* is a feature of the collaterals derive this interpretation from *takallalahu ᵓl-nasab ay taṭarrafahu,* i.e., kinship surrounds the deceased, that is, it is attached to him as he lacks the two utmost parts *walad* and *wālid.*[50] In Ibn al-Aṯīr, father and son are said to be the two utmost parts of a man.[51] The absence of the two utmost parts makes a person become a *kalāla.*[52] The heirs, except *wālid* and *walad,* encircle the kin of a deceased person, according to their proximity, the nearest first.[53] What surrounds (*iḥtaffa*) something on its sides (*ğawānib,* lateral lines, flanks) is *iklīl;* and a deceased person is named *kalāla* because the heirs encircle (surround) him (*yuḥīṭūna bihi*) on his sides.[54] *Kalāla* is assimilated to a person whose utmost parts (both extremities), that is his father and his *walad,* have fallen off; thus he has become feeble and dim, i.e., lacking lineage (direct relation).[55] The verse by al-Farazdaq is especially appropriate to this derivation.[56]

Kalāla *infinitive of* kalla/yakillu: *thus a person with neither* walad *nor* wālid

The definition of *kalāla* given by those who refer it to the deceased is confirmed by the etymology of the Arabic root *k-l-l.* The most ancient scholar, al-Ḫalīl b. Aḥmad (d. 175/791), considers *kalāla* as the infinitive

[49] See *EI²*, II, 807; *GAS,* I, 8.

[50] *Ğamhara,* I, 120; *Lisān,* XI, 592; *Muḥkam,* VI, 410; *Nihāya,* IV, 31; *Qāmūs,* IV, 45; *Tāğ,* VIII, 101; *Tāğ luġa,* II, 236.

[51] *Nihāya,* IV, 31. *Lisān* (XI, 594) and *Tāğ* (VIII, 102) have: "Ibn al-Aṯīr said: . . . ," attributing this statement directly to him. However Ibn al-Aṯīr, in his *Nihāya* (IV, 31), has: "It is said: . . . (*qīla*)"; thus, it is not his own statement.

[52] *Lisān,* XI, 594; *Tāğ,* VIII, 102.

[53] *Tahḏīb luġa,* IX, 447. It is repeated in *Lisān,* XI, 592, *Šarḥ Nīl,* VIII, 299, and *Tāğ,* VIII, 101.

[54] *Aḥkām Qurᵓān,* I, 448; *Durr,* IV, 32; *Ğāmiᶜ Ibn Baraka,* II, 570, 594; *Lisān,* XI, 594; *Mabsūṭ,* XXIX, 153; *Mağmaᶜ,* II, 16, 17; *Nihāya,* IV, 31–32; *Šarḥ Nīl,* VIII, 299; *Tafsīr Manār,* IV, 422; *Tafsīr Nīsābūrī,* IV, 201; *Tafsīr Ṭūsī,* III, 135–36. Howell, in his *Grammar* (Part II, 264), has said: "تكلل: it became an إكليل fillet, i.e., encircling."

[55] *Tahḏīb luġa,* IX, 447. It is repeated in *Lisān,* XI, 592, and *Tāğ,* VIII, 101.

[56] *Mabsūṭ,* XXIX, 153.

of the verb *kalla/yakillu.*[57] Another ancient scholar, al-Layṯ b. al-Muẓaffar (d. 190/805), comparing the term *kalāla,* as "a person who has neither *walad* nor *wālid,"* with the word *kall,* says that both are infinitives of the verb *kalla/yakillu* (*kall*^{an}, *kalālat*^{an}),[58] which means "to become exhausted, weak." This etymology was emphasized by Ibn Barrī al-Miṣrī[59] (d. 582/1187). He repeats that *kalāla* is originally the infinitive of *kalla/yakillu* (*kalla al-mayyit, kall*^{an}, *kalālat*^{an}), and that a deceased person becomes feeble if he has died leaving neither *walad* nor *wālid* as heirs.[60] Lastly, a confirmation of this etymology is also given by al-Zabīdī (d. 1205/1791), who says that "fundamentally (*fī ʾl-asās*) and by interpretation (metaphorically, *min al-maǧāz*), *kalāla* is a person who has neither *wālid* nor *walad,* i.e., a person who is feeble (*kalla ʿan*) because he does not have a contiguous kinship line (*qarāba mumāssa*)."[61]

Kalāla *synonymous with* tabāʿud: *remote kinship*

The distance from the original sense of the term is more evident in another etymology (*ištiqāq*) found in al-Saraḫsī,[62] and later repeated in some *tafsīrs.*[63] The verb *kalla,* according to this view, would be synony-

---

[57] *ʿAyn,* V, 279.The Ibāḍī work *Ǧāmiʿ Ibn Baraka* (II, 570) states that this meaning seems to be more linguistically appropriate. This is also the original derivation, according to another Ibāḍī text, *Šarḥ Nīl* (VIII, 298); it is because the deceased is feeble, since he has no *ʿaṣaba,* but only maternal relatives, to inherit from him.

[58] *Lisān,* XI, 592; *Maǧmaʿ,* II, 16; *Muḥkam,* VI, 410; *Tafsīr Manār,* IV, 422; *Tafsīr Nasafī,* I, 212; *Tafsīr Nīsābūrī,* IV, 201; *Tafsīr Rāzī,* II, 378; *Tafsīr Ṭūsī,* III, 136; *Tāǧ,* VIII, 101; *Tāǧ luġa,* II, 235.

[59] *Aʿlām,* IV, 200; *EI*^{2}, III, 733; *GAL,* I, 365, no. 2; S, I, 529–30, no. 2; *GAS,* VIII, 217, 218; *Tāǧ,* I, 13.

[60] *Lisān,* XI, 593; *Qāmūs,* IV, 45; *Šarḥ Muwaṭṭaʾ,* III, 105; *Tāǧ,* VIII, 101.

[61] *Tāǧ,* VIII, 102. M. Ullmann (*Wörterbuch der klassischen arabischen Sprache,* I, [Weisbaden, 1970], p. 291) relates three meanings of the fifth form "*takallala*"; two of them represent its ordinary sense: "(auf-)leuchten, sich lächelnd zeigen, lächeln/to light (up), to show oneself smiling, to smile"; and "gekrönt werden, sich krönen mit/to be crowned, to crown oneself with." The third meaning has a reference to kinship: "jd. umgeben (eigtl. nur von d. Seitenverwandtschaft) /to surround a p. (strictly only of collateral relatives)." For the first form *"kalla"* Ullmann gives only its usual meaning: "müde, erschöpft, abgespannt, schlapp sein oder werden/to be or become weary, fatigued, exhausted, weak (syn. *a*ʿyā)" (p. 288); "trübe, matt, blöde sein oder werden/to be or become dull, dim, languid" (p. 289).

[62] *Mabsūṭ,* XXIX, 153.

[63] *Aḥkām Qurʾān,* I, 448; *Tafsīr Manār,* IV, 422; *Tafsīr Rāzī,* II, 378.

mous with the verb *tabāʿada:* "to be separated, lie apart, lie at some distance from one another, to separate. . . ."[64] This is the case when there is neither *walad* nor *wālid,* because no direct link exists between a person and his relative, but such a relation is remote; thus, a distant kinship (*al-qarāba al-baʿīda*) is named *kalāla.* The verse of the anonymous poet, in al-Saraḫsī's version,[65] is especially appropriate in connection with this meaning.

As far as the definition of the term *kalāla* is concerned, we can accept the statement of the author of *Tahḏīb al-luġa,* al-Azharī, as sound, that "from the linguistic point of view and in accordance with the revelation and the *Sunna,* it means the same to say: every person who has died leaving neither *wālid* nor *walad* is the *kalāla* of his heirs; or, every heir, except *wālid* and *walad* of a deceased person, is the *kalāla* of the deceased."[66] Accordingly the etymology of *kalāla* changes, although considering it a synonym of *tabāʿud,* as found in later sources, seems nothing but a way to confirm that *kalāla* refers to distant kinship. It is not without significance that this view is related by the Ḥanafī jurist al-Saraḫsī, whose school agrees with the opinion that *kalāla* means collaterals,[67] as the Kūfan linguists examined above, al-Farrāʾ and Ṯaʿlab, also maintain, while the definition of the Kūfan Ibn al-Aʿrābī is not wrong but only partial. As regards the linguistic school of Baṣra, it consistently developed the meaning of *kalāla* as feebleness. In fact, the Baṣran scholars, despite the strange definition given by Abū ʿUbayda and al-Aḫfaš, and Abū ʿUbayd's propensity to agree with and elucidate the definition given by the Kūfan al-Aʿrābī, used *kalāla* to refer to a person who has died leaving neither ascendants nor descendants, the wealth and pillar of a patriarchal institution such as the Arab family.

---

[64] Cf. Wehr.

[65] See chapter one.

[66] *Tahḏīb luġa,* IX, 448. It is repeated in *Lisān,* XI, 592–93.

[67] See chapter five.

CHAPTER THREE

ḤADĪṮ LITERATURE: DEFINITION OF *KALĀLA*

In order to discover the most ancient debate regarding the term *kalāla* and the related doctrines, it is more important to study the *ḥadīṯ* literature than to analyze the teaching of the juridical schools.[1] The examination of this material allows us to identify the centers where *ḥadīṯ*s originated, and the uses to which the scholars put them in order to create a basis for their doctrine, and the growth of *isnād*s and *matn*s in some cases. I assume, first, that the *ḥadīṯ* materials reflect a debate that preceded the doctrinal systematization made by the Medinese (Mālik) and the Iraqi schools (Abū Ḥanīfa, Abū Yūsuf, al-Šaybānī) and that was concluded in the second half of the second century H. Secondly, I assume that one cannot adopt any general criterion in order to date a *ḥadīṯ* and that dating a *ḥadīṯ* in itself does not seem to be an overriding question. I shall only try to identify the tendency emerging from each *ḥadīṯ*. For the sake of convenience, but without any claim of certainty, I have made use of Schacht's proposition that "the existence of common transmitters enables us to assign a firm date to many traditions and to the doctrines represented by them."[2]

As far as the *ḥadīṯ* literature is concerned, I have examined the main collections of traditions. Some of them do not have any tradition on *kalāla,*[3] while others do take up the question.[4]

In the wealth of *ḥadīṯ* literature on *kalāla* one must distinguish two main positions. A group of traditions, which are the majority, reflecting the Medinese and Meccan doctrine, maintain that the meaning of the term *kalāla* is uncertain; while another smaller group of traditions, with Iraqi *isnād*s, give the term a precise meaning. Nothing was known from the Prophet on *kalāla,* as al-Saraḫsī writes[5]; but the Companions, and those after them, diverged on its interpretation.

---

[1] Very few indications can be found in *Concordance,* VI, 50–51.

[2] *Origins,* 175.

[3] *Musnad Abī Ḥanīfa, Musnad Ḥumaydī, Musnad Šāfiʿī.*

[4] *Muṣannaf, Muṣannaf Ibn a. Šayba, Musnad Dārimī, Musnad Ibn Ḥanbal, Musnad Ṭayālisī, Ṣaḥīḥ Buḫārī, Ṣaḥīḥ Muslim, Sunan Bayhaqī, Sunan Dāraquṭnī, Sunan Ibn Māǧa, Sunan Siǧistānī, Sunan Tirmiḏī.*

[5] *Mabsūṭ,* XXIX, 151.

IRAQI SCHOOL

We may summarize the views of the Iraqi School under the following two categories:

a) Iraqi doctrine: *al-kalāla man lā walad lahu wa-lā wālid*

b) Iraqi opposition: Muḥammad b. Sīrīn al-Baṣrī (d. 110/729), al-Ḥakam al-Kūfī (d. 113/731–32), Šuᶜba al-Baṣrī (d. 160/776–77)

The Iraqi doctrine is generally attributed to Abū Bakr. He is supposed to have said: "*Kalāla* is a person who has died leaving neither *walad* nor *wālid*"[6] (*isnād* 1). The majority of the Companions (for example, ᶜAlī, Zayd, and Ibn Masᶜūd, in addition to Abū Bakr) agreed on this definition, it is the position of the great mass of scholars, and it was handed down on the authority of Ibn ᶜAbbās.[7]

The *isnād* is wholly Kufan: Sufyān al-Ṯawrī al-Kūfī (d. 161/777–78), Ǧābir b. Yazīd al-Kūfī[8] (d. 127/744–45), and, lastly, al-Šaᶜbī al-Kūfī[9] (d. 103/721–22), a Successor and an authority of the Kūfans who in no way could have known Abū Bakr. His *ḥadīṯ* is *mursal* with respect to ᶜUmar, ᶜAlī, ᶜĀᵓiša, Ibn ᶜUmar, Ibn Masᶜūd, Muᶜāḏ, and others; and all the more so from Abū Bakr. The assessment of Ǧābir, likewise, is generally negative; he is considered one of the most *kaḏḏāb* (mendacious) of narrators, for instance, by Abū Ḥanīfa. Moreover, in the *Tahḏīb* under "Ǧābir"[10] and "al-Šaᶜbī"[11] we do not find that Ǧābir related on the authority of al-Šaᶜbī, but that Sufyān al-Ṯawrī related directly from him.[12]

---

[6] *Muġnī* (VII, 5) and *Tafsīr Nīsābūrī* (IV, 200) attribute this definition to Abū Bakr, without an *isnād. Šarḥ Nīl* (VIII, 298) relates the same definition without an *isnād.* The Sunnī *mufassir* al-Rāzī (*Tafsīr Rāzī,* II, 378) attributes to Abū Bakr the Šīᶜī definition: *man siwā ᵓl-wālidayni waᵓl-walad.*

[7] *Mabsūṭ,* XXIX, 152. *Tafsīr Ṭūsī* (III, 135) and *Maǧmaᶜ* (III, 17) quote Abū Bakr, Ibn ᶜAbbās, Ibn Zayd, Qatāda, al-Zuhrī, and Abū [text: Ibn] Isḥāq (not quoted in *Maǧmaᶜ,* ibid.); introducing some confusion, they include also ᶜUmar in this list.

[8] *Tahḏīb,* II, 46–51, no. 75.

[9] *Faqīh* and one of the most learned men of his time. Al-Šaᶜbī transmitted the *farāᵓiḍ* from ᶜAlī, but he drew them only by analogy from his statements; *Tahḏīb,* V, 65–69, no. 110.

[10] Cf. II, 46–51, no. 75.

[11] Cf. V, 65–69, no. 110.

[12] Cf. ibid., 66. However, the extremely negative appraisal of Ǧābir was perhaps based on the fact that he was counted among the Sabians and that he supported the doctrine of *raǧᶜa* (reincarnation); he believed that ᶜAlī would return to this world. He belonged to the extreme Šīᶜa and was considered a

We may infer that the reference to Abū Bakr was a pretext to give more authority to the Iraqi definition than to the Medinese one, ascribed to ᶜUmar, an authority later than Abū Bakr. The saying attributed to Abū Bakr was presumably put in circulation in the first half of the second century H., and the *matn* relates a definition that the Kūfans agreed on at that time.

Another Iraqi report reveals a dispute between the Medinese and the Iraqi, Kufan, and also the Baṣran schools. "Following his own *raʾy,* Abū Bakr said: '*Kalāla* is he who has (died leaving) neither *walad* nor *wālid.*' But ᶜUmar said: '*Kalāla* is (the deceased) who has no *walad.*' Then, ᶜUmar, when he was stabbed to death, said: 'I am ashamed before Allāh because I disagreed with Abū Bakr. I believe that *kalāla* is (the deceased) who has neither *walad* nor *wālid*'"[13] (*isnād* 2).

The common transmitter is ᶜĀṣim al-Baṣrī[14] (d. 141/758–59), who relates on the authority of al-Šaᶜbī al-Kūfī. Hence, according to the criterion of the common transmitter, we may deduce that this report was put in circulation in the first half of the second century H. The controversy emphasizes the pre-eminence of the Iraqi position because Abū Bakr chronologically precedes ᶜUmar. Likewise an attempt is made to make ᶜUmar agree with the Iraqi definition.

Rāfiḍī. He did not write down his *ḥadīṯs* and they were neglected; they were *matrūk.* Many Muslim critics considered Ǧābir as *kaḏḏāb* and very weak in *raʾy* and transmission (*riwāya*). For this reason, perhaps, it is said that Sufyān al-Ṯawrī did not belong to the school of Ǧābir and that he left out the reports of the *ḍuᶜafāʾ*. Cf. *Tahḏīb,* II, 46–51, no. 75.

[13] Also in *Tafsīr Manār* (IV, 423; VI, 106), *Tafsīr Nīsābūrī* (IV, 200) and *Tafsīr Rāzī* (II, 378), there are references to this report. In *Muṣannaf, Muṣannaf Ibn a. Šayba, Musnad Dārimī,* and *Tafsīr Ṭabarī* (nos. 8745–46), Abū Bakr states that he bases himself on his *raʾy.* Moreover, Ibn Abī Šayba has only Abū Bakr's definition, without any reference to ᶜUmar, while *Musnad Dārimī* and *Tafsīr Ṭabarī* (no. 8745) have the definition of Abū Bakr and this statement: "When ᶜUmar was appointed caliph, he said: 'I am ashamed before Allāh because I differed with him.'" *Tafsīr Ṭabarī* (no. 8747) attributes to Abū Bakr and ᶜUmar only the Iraqi definition, with the same chain of transmitters as in *Muṣannaf.* Lastly, *Mabsūṭ* (XXIX, 151–52) has a wider version of this *matn* and also combines it with *isnāds* 10, 11. It should be noted that Powers (pp. 22ff.) has likewise examined the *ḥadīṯ* literature reported in *Tafsīr Ṭabarī,* but in a rather different way.

[14] According to some Muslim critics, he is *ṯiqa,* but some others did not consider him as *ḥāfiẓ* (*Tahḏīb,* V, 42–43, no. 73).

Here the criticism expressed by the Ẓāhirī Ibn Ḥazm[15] (d. 456/1064) is important: first, if al-Šaᶜbī was born more than ten years after ᶜUmar's death, he obviously could have never known both Abū Bakr and ᶜUmar; thus, this is a *riwāya munqaṭiᶜa.* Secondly, it is a *riwāya bāṭila,* because it is well known that ᶜUmar differed with Abū Bakr.

A number of Baṣran[16] and Kūfan[17] authorities—Qatāda al-Baṣrī (d. 117/735), Maᶜmar al-Baṣrī (d. 152/769), ᶜAmr b. Šuraḥbīl al-Kūfī (d. 63/682–83), and Abū Isḥāq al-Kūfī (d. 126/743–44)—as well as the Medinese al-Zuhrī al-Madanī[18] (d. 124/741–42), agree on the definition of *kalāla* as (the deceased) who has neither *walad* nor *wālid* (*isnād* 3). The two *ḥadīṯ*s quoted in *Tafsīr Ṭabarī* make no reference to ᶜAmr b. Šuraḥbīl, but go directly to al-Zuhrī, Qatāda, and Abū Isḥāq. This means that the name of ᶜAmr was used only for corroboration. Further, it is quite impossible that al-Zuhrī, Qatāda, and Abū Isḥāq could have heard *ḥadīṯ* from ᶜAmr, because the temporal gap between them is too great. Hence the *isnād* is *munqaṭiᶜ* between them and ᶜAmr, and the *ḥadīṯ* may be presumed to have originated at the time of Qatāda, Abū Isḥāq, and al-Zuhrī, presumably in the first half of the second century H.

The presence of the Medinese al-Zuhrī in this context is not surprising, because he represents the Medinese opposition to the "living tradition" of the school; in fact, he did not agree with his school on the position of the grandfather. Rather, he believed that the grandfather has precedence over the brother in inheritance as well as in patronage, as the Ḥanafīs do.[19] Consequently, he followed the Iraqi definition of *kalāla,* too. This shows that the question of the grandfather and the interpretation of the word *kalāla* are linked.

In some *ḥadīṯ*s the perfect *isnād* vanishes, and we find the Iraqi definition attributed directly to some preeminent Iraqi scholars, such as al-Ḥakam al-Kūfī (d. 113/731–32) (*isnād* 4, *Tafsīr Ṭabarī,* no. 8761), al-

---

[15] *Muḥallā,* IX, 298.

[16] Qatāda attached the *isnād*s to the reports transmitted by him; thus we can date the use of the *isnād* at his time and we can explain why he is the common transmitter in *isnād*s 3, 9. On Qatāda, see *Ǧarḥ,* III_2, 133–35, no. 756; *Ḥuffāẓ,* 47–48, no. 104; *Ṭabaqāt,* II_2, 1; *Taḏkira,* I, 122–24, no. 107.

[17] ᶜAmr b. Šuraḥbīl al-Kūfī: *ṯiqa;* cf. *Tahḏīb,* VIII, 47, no. 78.

[18] *EI,* VIII, 1239–41; *GAL,* I, 64–65, no. 2; S, I, 102, no. 2; *Ǧarḥ,* IV, 71–74, no. 318; *GAS,* I, 280–83, no. 11; *Ḥuffāẓ,* 42–43, no. 95; *Isᶜāf,* 26; *Ṭabaqāt,* II_2, 135–136; *Taḏkira,* I, 108–13, no. 97.

[19] *Dir. ered. II,* 457.

Suddī al-Kūfī[20] (d. 127/744–45) (*isnād* 5), and the Medinese Ibn Zayd[21] (*isnād* 6). But the Medinese position is also attributed to al-Ḥakam (*isnād* 4): "*Kalāla* is a person who has neither *walad* nor a father."[22] Šuᶜba al-Baṣrī (d. 160/776–77), the common transmitter, is presumably at the origin of this *ḥadīṯ;* moreover, Šuᶜba himself reports the Medinese position in another *ḥadīṯ,* where he makes an addition regarding the Medinese definition (cf. *isnād* 12). Because of this, we may suppose that he represents the Iraqi opposition.

MEDINESE SCHOOL

It is possible to consider Medinese views under the following two headings:

a) Medinese doctrine: *al-kalāla man lā walad lahu wa-lā ab*
b) Medinese opposition: al-Zuhrī al-Madanī (d. 124/741–42), Ibn Zayd

"Nothing was so problematic among the Companions of the Messenger of Allāh as the question of *kalāla*"[23] (*isnād* 7). The *matn* clearly reveals the real situation. This *ḥadīṯ* does nothing if not to highlight the state of doubt and the lack of a clear-cut definition in Egyptian circles. As the transmitters of this report were connected to Medina and Mecca, it represents the Egyptian adoption of the uncertain Ḥiǧāzī position. The *matn* is pronounced by ᶜUqba (who died at the end of the caliphate of Muᶜāwiya),[24] then Marṯad al-Miṣrī[25] (d. 90/708–9), then the common link Yazīd al-Miṣrī[26] (d. 128/745). Thus this *ḥadīṯ* presumably originated in the first decades of the second century H. Thereafter the report is related through two channels: a) Saᶜīd b. Abī Ayyūb al-Miṣri[27] (d. 149/

[20] Al-Suddī wrote a *tafsīr* of the Qurᵓān, but it was not taken seriously. The opinions of the Muslim critics diverge on him; many of them consider al-Suddī negatively as *kaḏḏāb* or *ḍaᶜīf;* and his *ḥadīṯ* is not accepted as proof (*ḥuǧǧa*). *Tahḏīb,* I, 313–14, no. 572.

[21] *Ṯiqa;* his *ḥadīṯ* is accepted as juridical proof (*ḥuǧǧa*) (*Tahḏīb,* IX, 173–74, no. 257).

[22] *Muṣannaf Ibn a. Šayba;* or "*fa-huwa mā dūna ᵓl-ab*" (*Tafsīr Ṭabarī,* no. 8765).

[23] The *matn* is augmented in *Tafsīr Ṭabarī.*

[24] or, according to others, in the year 58/678 (*Tahḏīb,* VII, 242–44, no. 439).

[25] *Musnad Dārimī* has "Yazīd" instead of "Marṯad." He was a *muftī* of *ahl Miṣr* in his time and a *faqīh;* he is considered as *ṯiqa* (*Taḏkira,* I, 73, no. 68; *Tahḏīb,* X, 82, no. 142).

[26] *Tahḏīb,* XI, 318–19, no. 614; *GAS,* I, 341–42, no. 2.

[27] *Tahḏīb,* IV, 7–8, no. 9. He represents the intermediary through which the

766), and then ᶜAbd Allāh b. Yazīd al-Maqqarī[28] (d. 212/827–28); b) ᶜAbd Allāh b. Lahīᶜa al-Miṣrī[29] (d. 170/786–87). So, this *isnād* represents the best compromise between Medina, Mecca, and Egypt.

Some *ḥadīṯ*s relating the Medinese position have complete Medinese *isnād*s, while others have a mixed *isnād;* but all of them focus solely on the lack of knowledge on the part of ᶜUmar about the meaning of the term *kalāla.* The most authoritative Medinese source, *al-Muwaṭṭaʾ*, has a unique *ḥadīṯ* with a peculiar *isnād,* but its *matn* underwent many changes: "ᶜUmar b. al-Ḫaṭṭāb asked the Messenger of Allāh about *kalāla,* and the Messenger of Allāh said to him: 'The *āya* that was sent down in the summer at the end of the *Sūrat al-nisāʾ* is sufficient for you'"[30] (*isnād* 8).

This *ḥadīṯ* definitively shows, firstly, that in Medina any precise definition of *kalāla* was unknown, and, secondly, that the existence of a "family *isnad,*" the freedman Zayd b. Aslam al-Madanī[31] (d. 136/753–54) from his master ᶜUmar, is "not an indication of authenticity but only

---

science of *ḥadīṯ* was transferred from Medina to Egypt. He transmitted on the authority of *ahl al-Madīna,* while *ahl Miṣr* transmitted on his authority.

[28] Ibid., VI, 83–84, no. 165. He was considered Meccan. Originally from the region of Baṣra, he lived in Mecca, where he died.

[29] *GAS,* I, 94, no. 11; *Tahḏīb,* V, 373–79, no. 648.

[30] *Muwaṭṭaʾ*, III, 113, no. 1122. With the *isnād* Ibrāhīm al-Naḫaᶜī → al-Fuḍayl b. ᶜAmr → Mālik b. Miġwal → Abū Nuᶜaym, this *matn* is found in *Musnad Ibn Ḥanbal* (I, 38), with the addition: "I would prefer asking the Messenger of God about *kalāla* to possessing livestock of white breed," which appears in *Muṣannaf* (X, 302, no. 19184), *Musnad Ṭayālisī* (p. 12, no. 60) and *Sunan Ibn Māǧa* (II, 911, no. 2727). Ibn Saᶜd (*Kitāb al-Ṭabaqāt al-kabīr,* s.v. "ᶜUmar b. al-Ḫaṭṭāb" [III$_1$, 248, 256]), relates a statement of ᶜUmar according to which he decided (*aqḍā*) nothing about *kalāla.* A report (*Tafsīr Ṭabarī,* IX, 441, no. 10888) reflects to some extent the *matn* of the *Muwaṭṭaʾ*, but it is much enriched; however, its *isnād* is peculiar indeed (Masrūq → al-Ḥasan b. Masrūq → Ǧābir → Abū Ḥamza → etc.). I think it undoubtedly spurious, because Ǧābir b. Yazīd b. al-Ḥāriṯ al-Ǧuᶜfī was considered very weak (*ḍaᶜīf ǧidd^{an}*), while the name of al-Ḥasan b. Masrūq is unknown (see *Tafsīr Ṭabarī,* IX, 441–42, n. 3). Cf. a similar *ḥadīṯ,* on the authority of Saᶜīd b. al-Musayyib, in *Maǧmaᶜ* (II, 149), *Tafsīr Ṭabarī* (IX, 431, no. 10866), and *Tafsīr Ṭūsī* (III, 408, 411). *Tafsīr Manār* (IV, 423) relates a series of *ḥadīṯ*s attributed to ᶜUmar; but it states that these reports are unusual with respect to their contents (*hāḏihi ʾl-riwāyāt ġarība fī maᶜnāhā*). A similar negative judgment is expressed later on as well (VI, 107).

[31] *Tahḏīb,* III, 395–97, no. 728.

a device for securing its appearance,"[32] and, lastly, that "in tracing the history of the Medinese school of law, we must leave out of account ᶜUmar."[33] It is impossible for Zayd b. Aslam to have transmitted from ᶜUmar and for Mālik to have transmitted from Zayd b. Aslam. The temporal gap between them is considerable. This *ḥadīṯ* very likely reflects the situation at Mālik's time or slightly earlier; it originated at that time and represents Medina's "living tradition."

A variation of this *ḥadīṯ* is reported by many traditionists through the common transmitter Qatāda al-Baṣrī (d. 117/735): "ᶜUmar gave a *ḫuṭba* on Friday, he praised and glorified Allāh, and he said: 'O God! I did not leave anything more important than the question of *kalāla.* I asked the Messenger of God . . . till he jabbed my bosom (or my chest) with his finger[34] and said: "O ᶜUmar! The Verse of the Summer (4:176) that was revealed at the end of *Sūrat al-nisāʾ* is sufficient for you"'" (*isnād* 9).[35]

Two remarks are rather pertinent in this context. First, al-Saraḫsī infers from this *matn* that the Prophet referred ᶜUmar to Qurʾān 4:176 because he had to use his independent judgment (*iğtihād*) in determining its meaning in order that he might receive the reward of the *muğtahidūn;*[36] so the interpretation of *kalāla* here is based on *raʾy.* Secondly, in *Tafsīr Ṭabarī,*[37] there is an addition in the *matn;* ᶜUmar is to have said: *al-kalāla huwa mā ḫalā ʾl-ab,*[38] which is the Medinese definition. This statement was transmitted by Ibn ᶜArafa to al-Ṭabarī, while

[32] *Origins,* 170.

[33] Ibid., 243.

[34] or, till ᶜUmar leaned on his chest.

[35] The *matn* of this *ḥadīṯ* is inserted by al-Ṭayālisī (11, no. 53) and Ibn Ḥanbal (I, 27–28; 48–49) in a wider context that is yet wider in Ibn Ḥanbal (I, 15). Muslim, Ibn Māğa, and al-Bayhaqī, on the other hand, with some differences between them, relate only the section concerning our subject. Ibn Ḥanbal, further, in another place (I, 26), has a very concise *matn. Mabsūṭ* (XXIX, 151) relates a somewhat different text. Lastly, a short *matn* is given in *Tafsīr Manār* (VI, 104), and another *matn,* with considerable variations, is found later on in the same work (VI, 107).

[36] *Mabsūṭ,* XXIX, 151.

[37] no. 10877, with the *isnād:* Šuᶜba al-Baṣrī (d. 160/776–77) → Šabāba → Ibn ᶜArafa (d. 257/870–71). On Šuᶜba, see *Ğarḥ,* I_2, 369–71, no. 1609; *Ḥuffāẓ,* 83–84, no. 176; *Ṭabaqāt,* VII_2, 38; *Taḏkira,* I, 193–97, no. 187. On Šabāba, see *Ğarḥ,* I_2, 392, no. 1715; *Ṭabaqāt,* VII_2, 66; *Taḏkira,* I, 361, no. 352. On Ibn ᶜArafa, see *Ğarḥ,* II_2, 31–32, no. 128; *Ḥuffāẓ,* 134; *Taḏkira,* II, 502; *Tahḏīb,* II, 293–94, no. 523.

[38] *Aḥkām Qurʾān* (I, 653) has instead: *wa-huwa man lā walad lahu.*

Šabāba attributed it to Šu^c^ba; thus, the addition is peculiar to this chain of transmitters, but only from Šu^c^ba onwards. We may therefore suppose that Šu^c^ba al-Baṣrī was the originator of the addition, and hence we can deduce that Šu^c^ba represents the Iraqi opposition to the doctrine of his school.

Many other *ḥadīṯs* stress ^c^Umar's ignorance regarding *kalāla.* One of the devices used to this effect was a report that ^c^Umar had written a book on the grandfather and *kalāla* and that he had continued to ask Allāh for the proper inspiration. According to the report, ". . . when ^c^Umar was stabbed to death, he asked for the book and erased it. Therefore no one knew what it contained. Then he said: 'I wrote a book about the grandfather and *kalāla,* and I asked God for proper guidance in it; it is my opinion to let you remain in the doctrine you accept'" (*isnād* 10).[39]

The *isnād* is Medinese. As a matter of fact, Ma^c^mar al-Baṣrī[40] (d. 152/769), who was at Medina, relates on the authority of al-Zuhrī al-Madanī (d. 124/741–42). Al-Zuhrī relates on the authority of Sa^c^īd b. al-Musayyib al-Madanī[41] (d. 93/711–12), considered one of the most pre-eminent Successors. But it is doubtful whether he related on the authority of ^c^Umar. Most people believe that he did not know ^c^Umar; or that he met him at a very young age.

From this report I deduce, first, that the use of "grandfather" and "*kalāla*" in the same context means that the two questions are linked. Secondly, there was presumably no relation between ^c^Umar and Sa^c^īd. Furthermore, with reference to Sa^c^īd, I assume that we may agree with Schacht, when he writes that it is "impossible to regard information on the Medinese lawyers in the time of the Successors as genuine unless it is positively shown to be authentic. It would be rash to exclude this possibility *a priori,* but as far as I have been able to investigate the development of the Medinese doctrine, I have not found any opinion ascribed to one of these ancient lawyers which is likely to be authentic."[42] This being stated, we are confronted with the figure of al-Zuhrī. He did not agree with the Medinese doctrine on the grandfather, nor did he accept

[39] This *matn,* with some variations, is also found in *Tafsīr Manār,* IV, 423; VI, 106.

[40] *Taḏkira,* I, 190–91, no. 184; *Tahḏīb,* X, 243–46, no. 439.

[41] What is highly problematic is his relation with ^c^Umar. Some Muslim critics admit that he saw ^c^Umar and heard from him. But the prevailing opinion, followed also by Mālik, is that he did not know ^c^Umar, and that his *ḥadīṯs* from ^c^Umar are *mursal. Tahḏīb,* IV, 84–88, no. 145.

[42] *Origins,* 245.

the Medinese position on *kalāla;* in fact, he followed the Iraqi doctrine both on the grandfather and on the interpretation of *kalāla* (see *isnād* 3). Therefore, he represents the Medinese opposition to the "living tradition" of the school.[43] In conclusion, ᶜUmar's statement "it is my opinion to let you remain in the doctrine you accept" is evidence, at the beginning of the second century H., that in the Medinese school not all scholars were disposed to admit the innovation introduced in the doctrine regarding the grandfather based on the interpretation of *kalāla,* while the Iraqi doctrine represented continuity with the past. For this reason, I fully agree that "the conventional picture of Medina as the home of the *sunna* of the Prophet is artificial and late."[44] The doctrine of Medina as the "home of the *sunna* of the Prophet" seems to be nothing but an assertion created to cover precisely the opposite situation.

Another doubtful report, one of some length, would have it once again that the Prophet said nothing to ᶜUmar about *kalāla.* According to the report, the verse "Allāh informs you about *kalāla"* (Qurʾān 4:176) was sent down during a trip of the Prophet, and that Ḥuḏayfa b. al-Yamān[45] (d. 22/642–43), a secretary (*ṣāḥib sirr*) of the Prophet, was with him. The Prophet informed Ḥuḏayfa about this revelation, and Ḥuḏayfa informed ᶜUmar. When ᶜUmar was appointed caliph, he asked Ḥuḏayfa about the *tafsīr* of the verse; but the latter answered: "Oh (my) God! You are foolish if you believe that your office as caliph can make me to tell you what I did not tell you at that time"[46] (*isnād* 11).[47] Who could give more credibility to this report than Ḥuḏayfa, who was a contemporary of both the Prophet and ᶜUmar?

The *matn* was transmitted through two chains of *riǧāl,* but all of them are Baṣran. The first chain consists of Maᶜmar al-Baṣrī (d. 152/769), on the authority of Ayyūb al-Baṣrī[48] (d. 131/748–49), in his turn on the au-

---

[43] Ibid., 248.

[44] Ibid., 243.

[45] *Tahḏīb,* II, 219–20, no. 405.

[46] At the end of this *ḥadīṯ* in *Muṣannaf,* another *ḥadīṯ,* with the same *isnād,* directly on the authority of ᶜUmar, relates that he would say: "O God! Thou hast clarified the term *kalāla* to someone, but not to me." It seems as though ᶜUmar was apologizing for his ignorance about it.

[47] This *matn* is also related in *Aḥkām Qurʾān* (I, 653) and *Tafsīr Manār* (VI, 103–4). A reference to it is in *Maǧmaᶜ* (II, 149).

[48] *Ǧarḥ,* I_1, 255–56, no. 915; *Ḥuffāẓ,* 52, no. 115; *Isᶜāf,* 6; *Riǧāl,* 106, no. 34; 150, no. 160; *Ṭabaqāt,* VII_2, 14–17; *Taḏkira,* I, 130–32, no. 117.

thority of Muḥammad b. Sīrīn al-Baṣrī[49] (d. 110/729). The second consists of Ismā^cīl b. ^cUlayya al-Baṣrī[50] (d. 193/809) on the authority of Ibn ^cAwn al-Baṣrī[51] (d. 150/767).

Besides the singular answer Ḥuḏayfa gave to ^cUmar, considering he was speaking to a caliph, and since it seems he should have revealed any mystery concerning the circumstances of the revelation of Qur^ɔān 4:176, the report of this *ḥadīṯ* is contradicted, not surprisingly, by several other *matns*. These relate that the verse was revealed in the house of Ǧābir b. ^cAbd Allāh[52] (d. 73/692–93) during his illness, or in any case that it was revealed with reference to the inheritance of Ǧābir's daughters.[53]

The Muslim commentators themselves doubt the authenticity of this report, either because the *isnād* is *munqaṭi^c* between Ibn Sīrīn and Ḥuḏayfa or because the *ḥadīṯ* is known only on the authority of Ḥuḏayfa.[54] Ibn Sīrīn was born two years before the end of the caliphate of ^cUṯmān. Thus, it is impossible to imagine a contact between him and ^cUmar and Ḥuḏayfa. Given that Ibn Sīrīn (d. 110/728–29) is the common link, this *ḥadīṯ* was presumably put into circulation at about the end of the first century or at the beginning of the second, and it may be indicative of the Baṣran opposition to the Iraqi doctrine.

---

[49] *Tahḏīb,* IX, 214–17, no. 336.

[50] *Fihrist,* 317; *Ǧarḥ,* I_1, 153–55, no. 513; *Ḥuffāẓ,* 133–34, no. 290; *Ṭabaqāt,* VII_2, 70; *Taḏkira,* I, 322–23, no. 303. Sezgin (*GAS,* I, 112, no. 61) simply quotes his name.

[51] Cf. *Taḏkira,* I, 156–57; *Tahḏīb,* V, 346–49, no. 600.

[52] *Tahḏīb,* II, 42–43, no. 67.

[53] The *ḥadīṯ* of Ǧābir regarding the circumstances of the revelation of Qur^ɔān 4:176 is quoted by Ibn Ḥanbal (III, 298) with the variant: "No one inherits from me except *kalāla.*" Muslim quotes one (XI, 56) of five *ḥadīṯ*s from Ǧābir with the variant: "*Kalāla* inherit from me." This variant is lacking in the *ḥadīṯ*s quoted in al-Ṭayālisī (pp. 237, no. 1709; 240, no. 1742), al-Buḫārī (XXIII, 153; 165–66), Muslim (XI, 54–56), Ibn Māǧa (II, 911, no. 2728), Abū Dāwūd al-Siǧistānī (III, 79, nos. 2886–87), and al-Tirmiḏī (III, 282). The *ḥadīṯ* of Ǧābir is also quoted in *Aḥkām Qur^ɔān,* I, 652–53; *Maǧma^c,* II, 149; *Tafsīr Manār,* VI, 103; *Tafsīr Nasafī,* I, 267; *Tafsīr Nīsābūrī,* VI, 35; *Tafsīr Ṭabarī,* VIII, 33, no. 8730; 34, no. 8731; IX, 431–33, nos. 10867–69; *Tafsīr Ṭūsī,* III, 408. On the issue of where Qur^ɔān 4:176 was revealed (in Medina, according to the *ḥadīṯ* of Ǧābir, or on a trip, according to the *ḥadīṯ* of Ḥuḏayfa), cf. *Tafsīr Ṭabarī,* IX, 435–36; *Tafsīr Ṭūsī,* III, 407–8. *Tafsīr Manār* (VI, 104–5) believes that it is not the case that this verse was revealed on a trip.

[54] *Tafsīr Ṭabarī,* IX, 436, n. 3.

Another statement is attributed to ᶜUmar through two different channels. The Kūfan version (the Murǧiᵓite ᶜAmr b. Murra al-Kūfī,[55] d. 110/728–29 → Sufyān al-Ṯawrī al-Kūfī,[56] d. 161/777–78) (*isnād* 12) has: "It would mean more to me that the Prophet make clear three subjects: *al-ḫilāfa, al-kalāla,* and *al-ribā,* than that [I should possess] the world and what it contains." According to the Baṣran version (ᶜAmr b. Murra al-Kūfī → Šuᶜba al-Baṣrī), ᶜUmar said: "I would prefer to ask the Messenger of Allāh about three subjects: *al-ḫilāfa, al-kalāla,* and *al-ribā,* rather than possess livestock of white breed."[57]

However, the two versions differ in significant ways: in *Muṣannaf,* the *isnād* ends with ᶜAmr b. Murra, while in *Musnad Ṭayālisī, Sunan Ibn Māǧa, Tafsīr Ṭabarī,* and *Sunan Bayhaqī,* the name of Murra al-Kūfī[58] (d. 76/695–96) is added. Murra did not know ᶜUmar; his report from him is *mursal.*[59] Moreover, the Baṣran version has this addition: "Then I asked Murra: Who doubts that *kalāla* is all heirs except parent and child (*al-kalāla huwa mā dūna ᵓl-walad waᵓl-wālid*)? He answered: 'They doubt about *wālid.*'" Considering that ᶜAmr (d. 110/728–29) is the common link, at his time (at the beginning of the second century H.) the definition of *kalāla* was known, and even accepted, in Iraqi circles; moreover, ᶜAmr's statement that some people were doubtful about the inclusion of the *wālid* in the definition of *kalāla* clearly indicates the real divergence regarding the interpretation of the term *wālid.* Are we in presence of an Iraqi opposition to the doctrine of the school?

There is a Meccan version of the previous *ḥadīṯ,* but with a completely

---

[55] *Ǧarḥ,* III, 257–58, no. 1421; *Ḥuffāẓ,* 46, no. 102; *Ṭabaqāt,* VI, 220; *Taḏkira,* I, 121–22, no. 105.

[56] *Tahḏīb,* IV, 111–15, no. 199.

[57] Approximately this *matn* is also found in *Tafsīr Manār* (IV, 423), *Tafsīr Nīsābūrī* (IV, 200–201), and *Tafsīr Rāzī* (II, 378). Muslim (XVIII, 165) has two *ḥadīṯ*s with negligible variations in the *matn* and with the same last *raǧul*s in the *isnād:* ᶜUmar → Ibn ᶜUmar → al-Šaᶜbī → Abū Ḥayyān. The *matn* has a sentence regarding the prohibition of drinking wine. Then ᶜUmar simply states that he wished that the Messenger of Allāh had made clear to him three subjects: grandfather, *kalāla,* and *ribā.* A variation of this *ḥadīṯ,* with the same *isnād,* but without the reference to the prohibition of drinking wine, is in *Tafsīr Ṭabarī* (IX, 439, no. 10883) and *Sunan Bayhaqī* (VI, 245). Another *ḥadīṯ* (with the *isnād* ᶜUmar → Ibrāhīm al-Naḫaᶜī → al-Aᶜmaš → etc.) has this *matn:* "I would prefer to know something about *kalāla* than to have the equivalent of the *ǧizya* on the castles of Rūm" (*Tafsīr Ṭabarī,* IX, 439, no. 10881).

[58] *Tahḏīb,* X, 88–89, no. 158.

[59] Cf. *Tahḏīb,* X, 89.

different *isnād.* The *matn* seems to be a reworking of the previous one, with some additions. Instead of *ribā, zakā* is mentioned. ᶜUmar is reported to have said: "Rather than possess livestock of white breed, I would prefer to ask the Messenger of Allāh about three subjects: *al-kalāla, al-ḫilāfa* after the Prophet, and when someone says, 'We accept the *zakā* on our property but will not pay it to you,' whether killing them is lawful or not." He added: "The opinion of Abū Bakr was to kill them"[60] (*isnād* 13).

Ibn Ǧurayǧ[61] (d. 149/766) and ᶜAmr b. Dīnār (d. 125/742–43) were Meccan; Sufyān b. ᶜUyayna (d. 197/812–13) was a Kūfan; lastly, Muḥammad b. Ṭalḥa[62] (d. 111/729–30) was a Ḥiǧāzī. I can hardly believe that Muḥammad b. Ṭalḥa could refer to the authority of ᶜUmar; there is a great temporal gap between them. This *ḥadīṯ* originated probably in Meccan circles about the end of the first century or at the beginning of the second century H., and it represents the position of the school, which was similar to that of Medina.

A spurious *ḥadīṯ* (*isnād* 14) was transmitted through two channels. In *Muṣannaf Ibn a. Šayba* and *Tafsīr Ṭabarī* the Iraqi definition (*mā ḫalā ʾl-walad waʾl-wālid*) is attributed to ᶜUmar, while in *Sunan Bayhaqī* ᶜUmar is reported to have said: *al-kalāla man lā ab lahu wa-lā walad,* in accordance with the Medinese definition. I infer that Wakīᶜ al-Kūfī (d. 196/811–12) tried to attribute the Iraqi definition to ᶜUmar. This inference is wholly justifiable, since Wakīᶜ's reputation was not very high among Muslim critics: he made mistakes (*aḫṭaʾa*) in 500 *ḥadīṯ*s and he changed the pronunciations of *ḥadīṯ*s to imply new meanings.[63] Further-

---

[60] It is to be noted that ᶜAmr b. Dīnār and Ibn ᶜUyayna were accused or suspected of being Šīᶜī. So we can explain their reference to *zakā* rather than to *ribā.* ᶜUmar is made to raise the question of the duty to pay the *zakā* to the legitimate caliph. And ᶜUmar refers to the doctrine of Abū Bakr, the caliph who preceded him. It seems evident that the objection to paying the *zakā* comes from Šīᶜī circles and that the Sunnī answer is exactly that attributed to Abū Bakr. We may conclude that this *ḥadīṯ* suggests that, at the time of ᶜAbd al-Razzāq, the compiler of the *Muṣannaf,* the divergences between Sunnīs and Šīᶜīs had not yet led to a radical break between them on the religious level.

[61] He counterfeited traditions (*tadlīs*), and some Muslim critics considered him as completely weak (*ḍaᶜīf kulluhu*), while some others attributed to him the qualities of *ṯiqa, ṣadūq. Ḥuffāẓ,* 74, no. 157; *Taḏkira,* I, 169–71, no. 164; *Tahḏīb,* VI, 402–6, no. 855.

[62] *Tahḏīb,* IX, 239–40, no. 381.

[63] Ibid., XI, 123–31, no. 211.

more, there is a break in temporal continuity (*inqiṭāᶜ*) between Wakīᶜ and ᶜImrān al-Baṣrī (d. 149/766).[64] It would stand to reason then that Wakīᶜ counterfeited his report.

As far as Ḥammād b. Salama al-Baṣrī[65] (d. 167/783–84) is concerned, he reports the correct Medinese definition and may thus represent the Iraqi opposition. Perhaps he was the originator of his report, since not all Muslim critics agree on his reliability. The preceding narrator, ᶜImrān b. Ḥadir, was considered as *ṯiqa;*[66] but the first figure in the *isnād,* Sumayṭ b. ᶜUmayr al-Baṣrī, had no reliability because he maintained that ᶜUmar considered the grandfather like the father,[67] whereas we know that in the Medinese school a different doctrine was attributed to him, or, at least, that his position was uncertain.[68]

The *matn* in *al-Muwaṭṭa*ᵓ is quite literally repeated in a group of reports on the authority of al-Barāᵓ b. ᶜĀzib al-Madanī (d. 72/691–92) (*isnād* 15): "A man went to the Messenger of Allāh asking him about *kalāla.* He answered: 'The Verse of the Summer is sufficient.'"[69] The mention of al-Barāᵓ[70] gives great credibility to this report, which represents the Medinese position. The remaining transmitters are Kūfan.

This report underwent an unusual evolution and was in fact used for various purposes. There is no reference to *kalāla* in the *ḥadīṯ* with the *isnād* al-Barāᵓ → Abū ᵓl-Safar al-Kūfī[71] (d. 112/730–31) → Mālik b. Miġwal al-Kūfī[72] (d. 157/773–74); and also in al-Buḫārī,[73] Muslim,[74] al-Ṭabarī,[75] and al-Bayhaqī[76] it is only said that the last verse of the Qurᵓān

---

[64] Cf. *Muṣannaf Ibn a. Šayba,* n. 5.

[65] *Tahḏīb,* III, 11–16, no. 14. He sometimes added *isnād*s (*asnada*) to *ḥadīṯ*s that people related from him without a chain of transmitters.

[66] *Tahḏīb,* VIII, 125, no. 217.

[67] Ibid., IV, 240, no. 409.

[68] Cf. *Studies,* 6–10.

[69] It is also quoted in *Tafsīr Manār,* VI, 104.

[70] Cf. *Tahḏīb,* I, 425–26, no. 785. Al-Barāᵓ was Medinese, but he moved to Kūfa, where he died. He was a Companion of the Prophet and fought various battles together with him.

[71] Ibid., IV, 96–97, no. 162.

[72] Ibid., X, 22–23, no. 35.

[73] XXIII, 166.

[74] XI, 58–59, quoted five times. The *matn* reflects that of al-Buḫārī, with some negligible variations.

[75] *Tafsīr Ṭabarī,* IX, 433–34, nos. 10870–73.

[76] VI, 224.

to be revealed, which puts the seal on *Sūrat al-nisāʾ*, was 4:176.[77] Furthermore, Abū Dāwūd al-Siǧistānī quotes this *ḥadīṯ* twice. The first time,[78] with a completely different and totally new *matn*, al-Barāʾ states that another verse on *kalāla* was sent down, namely Qurʾān 4:12; while the second time[79] the *matn* acquires a significant addition: "Then I asked Abū Isḥāq al-Kūfī[80] (d. 126/743–44): 'Is *kalāla* a person who has died leaving neither *wālid* nor *walad*?' He answered: 'So they believe.'"

I infer that the original *ḥadīṯ* of al-Barāʾ, preserved in the chain Abū ʾl-Safar, etc., was reworked by Abū Isḥāq, the common link, with regard to *kalāla*, and, after him, it was also augmented by the addition of the Iraqi definition.

Another change in this *ḥadīṯ* is found in al-Ṭabarī[81] and al-Bayhaqī,[82] who, in the *isnād*, have Abū Salama b. ᶜAbd al-Raḥmān b. ᶜAwf al-Madanī (d. 94/712–13), instead of al-Barāʾ. Moreover, the *matn* is related on the authority of the Prophet. Al-Bayhaqī believes that the *ḥadīṯ* of Abū Isḥāq on the authority of Abū Salama is *munqaṭiᶜ* and not well known, while the known report is that of al-Barāʾ. Abū Salama did not hear *ḥadīṯ* from Abū Bakr, ᶜUmar, and others of their time.[83] He could hardly have known the Prophet.

MECCAN SCHOOL

Evolution of the position of the Meccan school from Medinese to Iraqi doctrine

The first stage of Meccan doctrine is represented by those reports related on the authority of Ibn ᶜAbbās that point to the ignorance of ᶜUmar concerning *kalāla*.[84] One such report is the following: "Ibn ᶜAbbās said: 'When he was struck down, ᶜUmar said to me: "Learn three things from me: . . , and about *kalāla* what, I said." I asked Ibn Ṭāwūs: "What did he

---

[77] This *matn* is also found in *Aḥkām Qurʾān*, I, 652; *Maǧmaᶜ*, II, 149; *Tafsīr Ṭūsī*, III, 407.

[78] III, 79, no. 2888.

[79] III, 79–80, no. 2889; quoted also by al-Bayhaqī.

[80] *Ǧarḥ*, III$_1$, 242–43; no. 1347; *Ḥuffāẓ*, 43–44, no. 97; *Riǧāl*, 64, no. 24; 71, no. 21; *Ṭabaqāt*, VI, 219; *Taḏkira*, I, 114–16, no. 99; *Tahḏīb*, VIII, 63–67, no. 100.

[81] *Tafsīr Ṭabarī*, IX, 442, no. 10889.

[82] *Sunan Bayhaqī*, VI, 224.

[83] *Tahḏīb*, XII, 115–18, no. 537.

[84] Cf. also *isnād*s 13, 18.

say?" But he refused to inform me'"[85] (*isnād* 16).

It is a *ḥadīṯ* of Meccan origin that underlines that nothing was known from ᶜUmar. Ibn ᶜAbbās,[86] then Ṭāwūs (d. 100/718–19 in Mecca), and subsequently Ibn Ṭāwūs (d. 131/748–49) are mentioned in the *isnād.* This is the typical Meccan *isnād.* The last transmitter is the Baṣran Maᶜmar (d. 152/769), but he stayed in Medina and al-Yaman and related on the authority of Ibn Ṭāwūs. We may conclude that at the time of Maᶜmar, the Meccan position is the same as that of Medina.

Another report used to show Meccan acceptance of the Medinese doctrine is one on the authority of Ibn ᶜAbbās according to which ᶜUmar made a *waṣiyya* on his deathbed. He said: *"Kalāla* is as I said." Ibn ᶜAbbās asked him: "What did you say?" He answered: "A person who has no *walad"*[87] (*isnād* 17).

---

[85] This *matn,* with variations, is also found in *Tafsīr Manār,* VI, 106. With a completely new *isnād,* but on the authority of Ibn ᶜAbbās, al-Ṭayālisī (pp. 6–7, no. 26) and Ibn Ḥanbal (I, 46), in a long *matn,* insert the fact that ᶜUmar did not establish anything about *kalāla.* Elsewhere, moreover, Ibn Ḥanbal (I, 20) has this statement of ᶜUmar inserted in a long context, but with a different *isnād.*

[86] With reference to Ibn ᶜAbbās, in the *Ṭabaqāt* (II_2, 120–21) it is related that the method he followed when he solved the juridical questions posed to him, was the following: The answer was based first on the Qurᵓān; if an appropriate verse was lacking, he based it on a Prophetic *ḥadīṯ;* if no *ḥadīṯ* existed on that problem, he had recourse to the authority of Abū Bakr and ᶜUmar; if neither caliph had solved such a problem, Ibn ᶜAbbās followed his own personal judgment (*raᵓy*). This report may be nothing but a temporal transposition. Such a method could not have been known in the time of Ibn ᶜAbbās. Yet it seems to have been applied to the case of *kalāla,* as nothing is in the Qurᵓān or in the *Sunna* of the Prophet; so opposite opinions are attributed to Abū Bakr and ᶜUmar, with precedence going to the first, as the Iraqis state. If this method had indeed been extant since the time of Ibn ᶜAbbās, the Medinese might have had to accept the Iraqi definition; but it is evident that it is a later device formulated by the schools in order to give authority to their doctrines.

[87] This *matn* is quoted in *Tafsīr Ṭūsī* (III, 135) and *Mağmaᶜ* (II, 17), where, however, there is *wālid,* instead of *walad* (see footnote in *Tafsīr Ṭūsī*). On the basis of this definition, Ibn ᶜAbbās makes the uterine brothers inherit one-sixth together with the parents. Ibn Ḥanbal (IV, 60) has a *ḥadīṯ* from Saᶜd regarding the *waṣiyya.* When Saᶜd asked the Prophet about the amount of the disposable portion of his estate for *waṣiyya,* he said: "I leave an inheritance as *kalāla."* This expression is lacking in the other analogous reports from Saᶜd related by Ibn Ḥanbal (I, 168, 171, 172 twice, 172–73 three times, 174, 176, 179, 181, 184) and by al-Buḫārī (XXIII, 160–61).

The Meccan Ibn Ǧurayǧ (d. 149/766) also gives a definition of *kalāla* that is Medinese. The circumstances of ᶜUmar's *waṣiyya* and the reported exchange between him and Ibn ᶜAbbās, however, seem rather improbable.

Another report stressing the acceptance of a common doctrine on the part of Medina and Mecca goes back to Ṭāwūs (d. 106?/724–25?), according to whom Ibn ᶜAbbās said: "I was the last person in the time of ᶜUmar who heard him say: '*Kalāla* is as I said.' I asked him: 'What did you say?' He answered: 'A person who has no *walad*'"[88] (*isnād* 18). The limitation of the *kalāla* to one who has no *walad* is the result of a strict interpretation, made by Ibn ᶜAbbās, of Qurᵓān 4:176, where only *walad* is quoted.[89] The *isnād* is Meccan: the first transmitter is the Kūfan Sufyān b. ᶜUyayna al-Kūfī[90] (d. 197/812–13); but he went to Mecca in the year 163/779–80, where he was in contact with Sulaymān b. Abī Muslim al-Aḥwal al-Makkī.[91] However, between the deaths of Sulaymān and Ṭāwūs there must have been a considerable time gap. A contact between them seems impossible. Maybe the name of Ṭāwūs was used only because he was considered a preeminent Meccan scholar, and the name of Ibn ᶜAbbās because he was the main reference for the Meccan doctrine. Probably this *ḥadīṯ* originated at the time of Sulaymān. Al-Bayhaqī doubts the authenticity of the report because it is unique (*infirād*) and because of evidence contained in various reports on the authority of ᶜUmar and Ibn ᶜAbbās. In any case, the Meccan school was aware of the Medinese position about *kalāla.* There is an addition only in *Muṣannaf:* "I believe that he [ᶜUmar] said: 'and no *wālid,*'" which is the Iraqi definition. This might be explained by the Meccan school having passed from the Medinese to the Iraqi definition, and because of the presence of the Kūfan Ibn ᶜUyayna in the *isnād.*

---

[88] *Mabsūṭ* (XXIX, 152) and *Baḥr* (V, 339) infer that, on the basis of such a definition, the uterine brothers/sisters inherit together with the parents. *Šarḥ Nīl* (VIII, 298), without an *isnād,* gives the definition of *kalāla* as a deceased person lacking *walad.*

[89] *Mabsūṭ,* XXIX, 152. But al-Saraḫsī (*Mabsūṭ,* XXIX, 152–53), based on a circumstantial analysis of the term *wilāda* and *ḏurriyya* (progeny), demonstrates that the term *walad* also includes the *wālid;* at the same time *ḏurriyya* includes *awlād* as well as *ābāᵓ*.

[90] According to some Muslim critics, he had some relations with the Šīᶜa; he was considered the most learned man among *ahl al-Ḥiǧāz* concerning *ḥadīṯ* (*Tahḏīb,* IV, 117–22, no. 205).

[91] Ibid., 218, no. 368.

Another means of marking the ignorance of ᶜUmar concerning *kalāla* was to use a sensational name, Ḥafṣa[92] (d. 27/647–48), his daughter, a wife of the Prophet. ᶜUmar ordered her to ask the Prophet about *kalāla*. . . . The Prophet said: "Did ᶜUmar order you to do this? I do not believe he will understand it. Is the Verse of the Summer not sufficient for him?" . . . ᶜUmar . . . said: "My God! Thou hast clarified the term *kalāla* to someone, but not to me"[93] (*isnād* 19).

The *ḥadīṯ* is of Meccan origin, but it was spread in Kūfa and Baṣra. It was transmitted through two channels. In one, Sufyān b. ᶜUyayna al-Kūfī (d. 197/812–13) related on the authority of ᶜAmr b. Dīnār al-Makkī[94] (d. 125/742–43), who related on the authority of Ṭāwūs[95] (d. 106?/724–25?). In the other, Maᶜmar al-Baṣrī (d. 152/769) related on the authority of Ibn Ṭāwūs[96] (d. 131/748–49), who related on the authority of his father. Using the usual criterion of the common transmitter, I may conclude that this *ḥadīṯ* presumably goes back to the end of the first century H., and that it represents the position of the Meccan school in conformity with that of Medina.

However, the Meccan doctrine changed, as some *ḥadīṯ*s on the authority of Ibn ᶜAbbās himself show, but the classical "family *isnād*" Ṭāwūs → Ibn Ṭāwūs significantly no longer appears. In fact, a *ḥadīṯ* (*isnād* 20) is related along two lines. With the *isnād:* ᶜAmr b. Dīnār al-Makkī (d. 125/742–43) → Ibn Ǧurayǧ al-Makkī (d. 149/766), al-Ḥasan b. Muḥammad b. ᶜAlī al-Madanī[97] (d. 99/717–18) said: "I heard Ibn ᶜAbbās say: '*Kalāla* is a person who has neither *walad* nor *wālid*.'" But with the *isnād* going through Ibn ᶜUyayna al-Kūfī (d. 197/812–13), there is an addition in the *matn* attributed to Ibn ᶜUyayna himself: "(Al-Ḥasan b. Muḥammad) said: 'I asked Ibn ᶜAbbās: "Allāh says '. . . If it is a man

---

[92] Different death dates are 41/661–62 or 45/665 (*Aᶜlām*, II, 292–93; *Ṭabaqāt kubrā*, VIII, 81–86; *Tahḏīb*, XII, 410–11, no. 2764).

[93] No. 19195 is reported in a very short form: "ᶜUmar ordered Ḥafṣa to ask the Prophet about *kalāla*." This *matn* is also found in *Tafsīr Manār* (IV, 423; VI, 104). *Mabsūṭ* (XXIX, 151; but, instead of ᶜUmar, Ibn ᶜUmar is named) has a more detailed text; further, it combines this *matn* with that of *isnād* 12 (but, instead of *al-ḫilāfa*, *al-ḫilāba* is given).

[94] He was suspected of being a Šīᶜī; but, according to al-Ḏahabī, this was false (*bāṭil*) (*Tahḏīb*, VIII, 28–30, no. 45).

[95] *Ǧarḥ*, I_2, 500–501, no. 2203; *Ḥuffāẓ*, 34, no. 77; *Isᶜāf*, 14; *Riǧāl*, 94, no. 3; *Ṭabaqāt*, V, 391–95; *Taḏkira*, I, 90, no. 79; *Tahḏīb*, V, 8–10, no. 14.

[96] *Ǧarḥ*, II_2, 88–89, no. 405; *Ṭabaqāt*, V, 397; *Tahḏīb*, V, 267–68, no. 458.

[97] *Tahḏīb*, II, 320–21, no. 555.

who dies, leaving a sister but no child (*walad*), she shall have half the inheritance; if [the deceased is] a woman, who leaves no child (*walad*), her brother takes her inheritance . . .'" (*Sūra* 4:176). But he rebuked me.'"[98]

Here Ibn ᶜAbbās follows the Iraqi definition. At the remark of al-Ḥasan reminding him of the literal reading of Qurᵓān 4:176, previously accepted by him, he rebuked him. This exchange seems nothing but a device to show that now the doctrinal position of the Meccan school no longer conforms to that of Medina represented by al-Ḥasan b. Muḥammad; it indicates the change in the Meccan doctrine and means that by Ibn ᶜUyayna's time the Meccan law school had definitively rejected the Medinese doctrine.

The change in the Meccan doctrine is so certain that some reports, through the common link Abū Isḥāq al-Kūfī (d. 126/743–44), simply attribute the Iraqi definition to Ibn ᶜAbbās[99] (*isnād* 21). Moreover, in four of these *ḥadīṯs,*[100] there is no reference to Ibn ᶜAbbās, the *isnād* stopping at Salīm,[101] who quotes the Iraqi definition and adds that they (who? the Meccans?) agree (*aǧmaᶜa*) with it. Here, too, the classical Meccan *isnād* Ṭāwūs → Ibn Ṭāwūs does not appear.

Based on the *ḥadīṯ* literature examined thus far, a first series of concluding remarks can be made. The debate on the definition of *kalāla* was based on *raᵓy*, as Mālik admits implicitly[102] and as some *ḥadīṯs* state ex-

---

[98] Qurᵓān trans. A. Yūsuf ᶜAlī, slightly altered; addition in parentheses mine. Al-Bayhaqī has only negligible variations, while Ibn Abī Šayba, al-Dārimī, and al-Ṭabarī quoted it in a simplified form: "*Kalāla* is the person who has neither *walad* nor *wālid.*"

[99] The Arabic text is wrong because it has: *mā ḫalā ᵓl-walad waᵓl-walad* instead of *mā ḫalā ᵓl-wālid waᵓl-walad.* Al-Bayhaqī has only the definition of Ibn ᶜAbbās.

[100] *Isnād* 21; *Tafsīr Ṭabarī,* nos. 8756–59.

[101] *Ṭabaqāt kubrā,* VI, 215.

[102] The Medinese doctrine concerning the grandfather was not based on *Sunna,* but on *raᵓy.* Such is exactly the interpretation given to the *ḥadīṯ* of Mālik by the Ḥanafī jurist al-Saraḫsī (*Mabsūṭ,* XXIX, 151), when he writes that the Prophet referred ᶜUmar to Qurᵓān 4:176 in order to make him use his personal judgment (*iǧtihād*) in determining its meaning so as to receive the reward of the *muǧtahidūn.* Mālik (*isnād* 8) refers only to Qurᵓān 4:176 and makes us understand that it is to be interpreted according to one's *raᵓy,* as al-Saraḫsī clearly points out in the commentary. Mālik expounds the method followed by his school in the interpretation of the term *kalāla* in the chapter "Inheritance of the

plicitly. Nothing was genuinely known from the Prophet. The Iraqi definition, attributed to Abū Bakr, represents continuity with the past, and it corresponds to that given by the majority of the linguists.

On the other hand, most of the reports regarding ᶜUmar and the Medinese position represent a rupture with the ancient doctrine; otherwise, if the reports were true, how could one explain that, insistently and in various ways, it is said that ᶜUmar related nothing on the subject? The Egyptian traditionists agreed with the Medinese teaching, while the Meccans came eventually to adhere to the Iraqi doctrine. Here Goldziher's theory that a *ḥadīṯ* is created in order to support a doctrine seems to be fully substantiated.[103]

Why was there recourse to *raʾy* in order to explain this word, and why did Muḥammad not feel the need to use his *raʾy*? It is possible that the meaning was very clear to him. Perhaps for a certain time after the Prophet's death there was no doubt regarding its meaning. The recourse to *raʾy* would thus conceal the need of the law schools to adapt the meaning to the requirements of a new doctrine, which would mean that no juridical school at that time respected the original meaning of the term *kalāla.* This brings us to imagine a legal doctrine that was originally connected with Qurʾān 4:12 and 4:176 and that was different from what was subsequently elaborated by the law schools.

The presence in the *isnād*s of *riǧāl* classified as Šīᶜī or Murǧiʾī or Qadarī or Rāfiḍī or followers of ᶜAbd Allāh b. Sabaʾ makes us understand that the complex debate was not only a Sunnī affair. Rather it was common to the various religious trends of that period, but without any sectarian bias. Only later was the distinction between Sunnīs and Šīᶜīs imposed. As a consequence, the Šīᶜīs, who for political reasons had become separated from the Sunnīs, created their own collections of *ḥadīṯ*s and their own juridical system, partly corresponding to the Sunnī one.

---

kalāla" (*Muwaṭṭaʾ,* III, 113–15). Mālik says: "The generally agreed-on doctrine among us, on which there is no divergence, and which I knew from the scholars in our country, is that *kalāla* is of two types" (*Muwaṭṭaʾ,* III, 113–14). Thus, the method is to distinguish Qurʾān 4:12 and Qurʾān 4:176. Also *Aḥkām Qurʾān* (I, 450–51) refers to the use of *iǧtihād.* The translation of the term *kalāla,* both in the relevant title and the text of *al-Muwaṭṭaʾ* made by Aisha Abdurrahman Bewley (see *Al-Muwatta of Imam Malik ibn Anas: The First Formulation of Islamic Law* [London and New York, 1989], 205), as "persons without parents or offspring" is wrong because it does not reflect the Mālikī view, but it is in accordance with the Ismāᶜīlī and Imāmī doctrine.

[103] See *Teorie,* 3–17.

The *ḥadīṯ* material shows that the debate moved from a mere definition of the term *kalāla* to its doctrinal implications. However the teachings were not altogether univocal among the scholars of the Iraqi and Medinese schools; inside each school there was an opposition. In the traditionist literature we find in an embryonic form what was later debated in the juridical schools. The question of the grandfather, which caused deep divergence between them, appears in the background. In this context, in order to prove the link between the two questions of the definition of *kalāla* and of the position of the grandfather in inheritance law, it is noteworthy, for instance, that al-Zuhrī, representing the doctrinal opposition in Medina, agrees with the Iraqi doctrine on both issues. Other evidence is the divergence between the Iraqi and Medinese schools regarding the definitions of *kalāla* found in the *ḥadīṯ* literature, which reflects their divergence regarding the grandfather. There is no doctrinal distinction between the two Iraqi cities of Kūfa and Baṣra on either question. The two main centers where the juridical debate developed were Iraq and Medina.

CHAPTER FOUR

ḤADĪṮ LITERATURE: *ᶜAṢABA MAᶜA ĠAYRIHI*

The *ᶜaṣaba maᶜa ġayrihi* (the agnate with another) are full or consanguine sisters when they survive together with daughters of the deceased and there are no other closer heirs.[1] Fyzee[2] correctly describes these cases as "anomalous." In fact, an agnate is only a male; thus, the true group of agnates including all male agnates is in Islamic law the *ᶜaṣaba bi-nafsihi,* the agnate in his own right. The law schools were forced to create the idea of the *ᶜaṣaba maᶜa ġayrihi* in order to justify their remarkable teaching. As a consequence, their interpretation of the term *kalāla* was also adapted to their purpose. The question involved was whether one or more full or consanguine sisters might inherit with one or more daughters, or female grandchildren *ex filio* when there are no other closer heirs. Both daughters and sisters are Qurᵓānic heirs; but, according to a strict interpretation of the Qurᵓān, daughters prevent sisters from inheritance. However, how could one allow the exclusion of the sisters in favor of other more distant kindred, given that sisters are Qurᵓānic heirs entitled to receive a great share of the estate? Hence the need to create the strange notion of the *ᶜaṣaba maᶜa ġayrihi.*

The succession of daughters inheriting together with full or consanguine sisters may be subdivided into two sections: 1) one or more daughters together with one or more sisters; 2) one daughter together with one or more son's daughters and one or more sisters.

For the first case, we find some *ḥadīṯs* that essentially support two doctrines; the majority of scholars consider the sisters as *ᶜaṣaba,* while a few deny this. Because of the scarceness of the divergences among the schools of law and the individual jurists on this subject, little data can be found about the origin of the doctrine of *ᶜaṣaba maᶜa ġayrihi.*

The central personage in this debate is Muᶜāḏ al-Madanī[3] (d. 17/638), who in al-Yaman divided an estate into two halves between a daughter and a sister (*isnād* 22). However, this report was subject to significant growth. Firstly, in some *matn*s, found in the most recent collections of

---

[1] See A. A. A. Fyzee, *Outlines of Muhammadan Law,* 2d ed. (London 1955), 359.

[2] *Ibid.*

[3] *Tahḏīb,* X, 186–88, no. 347.

ḥadīṯ,[4] there is the following addition: Muᶜāḏ decided thus "in the time of the Messenger of Allāh." But al-Buḫārī and al-Bayhaqī point out that this statement was not related by the transmitter Sulaymān, and thus it was due to Šuᶜba. A similar addition is in *Sunan Siǧistānī* (no. 2893) and in *Sunan Dāraquṭnī* (no. 50): "in the time when the Prophet was alive." Secondly, in *Sunan Dāraquṭnī* (no. 48) there is the addition: "Muᶜāḏ did not allow the *ᶜaṣaba* to inherit anything," which refers to the agnates more remote than brothers, because a condition for the case examined here is that full or consanguine brothers were not present. Further, it is obvious that father and sons were not present because they bar sisters from inheritance. Finally, in *Sunan Bayhaqī,*[5] the solution is no longer attributed to Muᶜāḏ, but to the Prophet himself. However, in *Muṣannaf Ibn a. Šayba*[6] there is no reference to Muḥammad. It is evident that the text in *Sunan Bayhaqī* represents an attempt to give more authority to the solution of the case by referring it directly to the Prophet.

The common link in the *isnād* of the unaugmented version is al-Aswad b. Yazīd al-Kūfī[7] (d. 74/693–94), from whom al-Ašᶜaṯ al-Kūfī[8] (d. 125/742–43), Ibrāhīm al-Naḫaᶜī[9] (d. 95/713–14), Abū Hišām, Abū Ḥassān al-Baṣrī[10] (d. 130/747), and al-Musayyib b. Rāfiᶜ al-Kūfī[11] (d. 105/723) related.

Following the criterion of the common transmitter, the solution might be traced back to an earlier period, but not to the time of the Prophet.

Another *ḥadīṯ* (*isnād* 23) simply reports Muᶜāḏ's decision, but in *Muṣannaf* (no. 19026) the name of al-Aswad does not appear. Could this be an indication that the *ḥadīṯ* was put in circulation only at the time of Ibn Sīrīn (d. 110/728–29), that is at about the end of the first century or at the beginning of the second century H.?

A series of *ḥadīṯ*s relate that many ancient scholars, representing the different ancient schools of law, agreed with Muᶜāḏ's doctrine.

---

[4] with the *isnād:* al-Aswad → Ibrāhīm → Sulaymān → Šuᶜba (*Ṣaḥīḥ Buḫārī,* XXIII, 165; *Sunan Bayhaqī,* VI, 233). The *matn* of this *ḥadīṯ* is also related, with some variations and additions, in *Aḥkām Qurʾān,* I, 452.

[5] VI, 233.

[6] no. 11116; with the same *isnād:* al-Aswad → Ibrāhīm → al-Aᶜmaš.

[7] *Tahḏīb,* I, 342–43, no. 625.

[8] *Ṭabaqāt,* VI, 223; *Tahḏīb,* I, 355, no. 647.

[9] *Ḥuffāẓ,* 29–30, no. 68; *Taḏkira,* I, 73–74, no. 70.

[10] His reliability is invalidated because he followed the opinion of the Ḫawāriǧ (*Tahḏīb,* XII, 72, no. 287).

[11] Ibid., X, 153, no. 291.

IRAQI SCHOOL

The Iraqi position is represented by two *ḥadīṯ*s, one from ᶜAbd Allāh b. ᶜUtba al-Kūfī[12] (d. 73/692–93) → Abū Ḥaṣīn al-Kūfī[13] (d. 127/744–45) → etc. (*isnād* 24), and another from al-Šaᶜbī al-Kūfī (d. 103/721–22) → Ǧābir b. Yazīd al-Kūfī (d. 127/744–45) → etc. (*isnād* 25). The first *ḥadīṯ* simply solves the case of a daughter and a full or consanguine sister inheriting together, while the second *ḥadīṯ* has a more extensive *matn*. Indeed, it informs us that it represents the doctrine of ᶜAlī, Ibn Masᶜūd, and Muᶜāḏ, and that it was the stated opinion of the Companions of the Prophet, except Ibn ᶜAbbās[14] (d. 68/687 in Ṭāʾif) and Ibn al-Zubayr al-Makkī[15] (d. 72/691–92), who denied it.

MEDINESE SCHOOL

The solution of dividing the estate into two halves between a daughter and a sister is attributed to ᶜUmar through an *isnād* that represents the Medinese-Egyptian position: Abū Salama al-Madanī (d. 94/712–13) → Yazīd al-Miṣrī (d. 128/745–46) → Yaḥyā al-Miṣrī (d. 168/784–85) (*isnād* 26). However Ibn Ḥanbal considered Yaḥyā to have had a bad memory (*sayyiʾ al-ḥifẓ*) and held his *ḥadīṯ*s to be *munkar*.[16] Based on Ibn Ḥanbal's opinion, and given that Yaḥyā is the common transmitter, we might conclude that the report was put in circulation in his time.

Another report indicating the Medinese position is attributed to Ibn Abī ʾl-Zinād al-Madanī (d. 174/790–91), relating the same doctrine as above (*isnād* 27), and thus representing the position of that law school in his time. However, Ibn Abī ʾl-Zinād also relates a doctrine of Zayd b. Ṯābit that stated: "Sisters inheriting together with daughters are considered as *ᶜaṣaba;* they are entitled to receive only the remainder" (*isnād* 28).

Some remarks seem appropriate here. First, there are two highly dubious "family *isnād*s": Ibn Abī ʾl-Zinād from his father Abū ʾl-Zinād al-Madanī[17] (d. 130/748), and Ḫāriǧa b. Zayd b. Ṯābit al-Madanī[18] (d.

---

[12] *Ǧarḥ,* II_2, 124, no. 569; *Riǧāl,* 23, no. 14; *Ṭabaqāt,* VI, 82; *Tahḏīb,* V, 211–12, no. 531.

[13] *Tahḏīb,* VII, 126–28, no. 269.

[14] *Ǧarḥ,* II_2, 116, no. 527; *Ḥuffāẓ,* 10, no. 18; *Isᶜāf,* 16; *Riǧāl,* 22; *Ṭabaqāt,* II_2, 119–24; *Taḏkira,* I, 40–41, no. 18.

[15] *Isᶜāf,* 16; *Tahḏīb,* V, 213–15, no. 371.

[16] *Taḏkira,* I, 227–28, no. 212.

[17] *Tahḏīb,* V, 203–5, no. 351.

[18] Ibid., III, 74–75, no. 143.

99/717–18) from his father Zayd b. Ṯābit al-Madanī[19] (d. 45/666). Secondly, Ḫāriǧa is counted among the seven *fuqahā*ʾ of Medina;[20] but "the concept of seven representative lawyers of Medina at the end of the first century has no foundation in fact."[21] Finally, Ibn Abī ʾl-Zinād was learned in the Qurʾān and traditions (*aḫbār*), and he gave *fatwās*. However, by the majority, he was considered weak; his *ḥadīṯ* was *muḍṭarib* and not taken as juridical proof. But the most important thing is that he was also weak in reports from his father, Abū ʾl-Zinād; Ibn Abī ʾl-Zinād was among those who wrote down *ḥadīṯ*.[22] This being the case, I may conclude that the report from Ibn Abī ʾl-Zinād is unreliable. Presumably he was its originator. It is possible that he expressed a generally accepted doctrine of his time as a juridical maxim.

MECCAN SCHOOL

The position of the Meccan school is more complicated. A series of *ḥadīṯ*s reveals the debate between the Meccan school and the remaining law schools, and then its acceptance of the common doctrine. An attack on the Medinese school (note in the *isnād* the presence of Abū Salama al-Madanī and al-Zuhrī al-Madanī) can be perceived in a *ḥadīṯ* in which Ibn ᶜAbbās denied the doctrine of *ᶜaṣaba maᶜa ġayrihi.* According to the *matn,* a man went to Ibn ᶜAbbās asking him about the solution of the case of a daughter and a full sister inheriting together. He gave one-half to the daughter and the remainder to the *ᶜaṣaba,* while the sister was excluded. But the man said to him that ᶜUmar had decided in a different way, dividing the estate into two halves between a daughter and a full sister. But Ibn ᶜAbbās rebuked him. Then the man met Ibn Ṭāwūs, who informed him, on the authority of his father Ṭāwūs, that Ibn ᶜAbbās gave this solution based on the literal interpretation of Qurʾān 4:176 ("If a person has died leaving no *walad,* a sister shall be entitled to receive one-half") (*isnād* 29), where *walad* includes both a male and a female child.

A transition from the negation of the doctrine of the *ᶜaṣaba maᶜa ġayrihi* to its acceptance is represented by a *ḥadīṯ* in which there is an attempt to hide the position of Ibn ᶜAbbās. Its *isnād* (*isnād* 30) is fully Meccan. However, two elements in the chain of transmitters give rise to

---

[19] *EI,* VIII, 1194–95; *Ǧarḥ,* I, 558, no. 2524; *GAS,* I, 395–96; *Ḥuffāẓ,* 8, no. 15; *Isᶜāf,* 10; *Ṭabaqāt,* II_2, 115–17; *Taḏkira,* I, 30–32, no. 15.

[20] *Tahḏīb,* III, 75.

[21] *Origins,* 243.

[22] *Tahḏīb,* VI, 170–73, no. 353.

many doubts about its authenticity and allow us to consider this *ḥadīṯ* as later than those traditions that attribute an opinion to Ibn ᶜAbbās. The *isnād* is perfect because it goes back to the Prophet, and Ibn ᶜAbbās and the Prophet are linked through an anonymous *rağul*. According to the *matn,* Ibn Ğurayğ al-Makkī (d. 149/766) asked Ibn Ṭāwūs about a daughter and a sister inheriting together. Ibn Ṭāwūs answered that his father, Ṭāwūs, remembered nothing about it based on the authority of Ibn ᶜAbbās. This account is clearly in contradiction with other reports.

A debate with the Kūfan school and an indication of the change in the Meccan position can be found in two *ḥadīṯ*s. In the first, it is said that Ibn al-Zubayr did not allot anything to a full sister inheriting together with a daughter until al-Aswad al-Kūfī informed him of the solution given by Muᶜāḏ for this case. Then Ibn al-Zubayr said to al-Aswad: "You are my emissary to ᶜAbd Allāh b. ᶜUtba," who was his *qāḍī* in Kūfa, "inform him of this decision" (*isnād* 31).

It must not escape us that this *isnād* is similar to some chains of *isnād* 22 (Muᶜāḏ's decision to divide an estate equally between a daughter and a sister), and that it reflects the chain of *isnād* 23 (Muᶜāḏ's decision again), as the transmitter Wabra al-Kūfī[23] (d. 116/734) is not mentioned in *Muṣannaf Ibn a. Šayba*[24] or in *Musnad Dārimī,*[25] where Ibrāhīm relates directly from al-Aswad. What is new here is that Meccan scholars agree with the Iraqi doctrine.

Likewise according to the second *matn* (*isnād* 32), the Meccan Ibn al-Zubayr changed his doctrine. This *ḥadīṯ* seems to represent a more elaborated version than the previous one (*isnād* 31). The persons are the same: Ibn al-Zubayr, ᶜAbd Allāb b. ᶜUtba, al-Aswad, Muᶜāḏ. The report is that al-Musayyib b. Rāfiᶜ al-Kūfī was sitting with ᶜAbd Allāh b. ᶜUtba and demanded of him to solve the case of a daughter and a sister inheriting together. Ibn al-Zubayr directed him to give nothing to the sister, and ᶜAbd Allāh b. ᶜUtba obeyed. At that moment al-Aswad said that he was present when Muᶜāḏ divided the estate into two halves between daughter and sister in al-Yaman. ᶜAbd Allāh b. ᶜUtba went to Ibn al-Zubayr and informed him of this. Then, Ibn al-Zubayr also agreed. The *matn* concludes saying that Abū Bakr as well divided an estate in halves between a daughter and a sister.

I believe that a report of this kind is simply a device to stress the doc-

[23] Cf. ibid., XI, 111, no. 194.
[24] no. 11118.
[25] no. 2883.

trinal change in the Meccan law school. Further, I think that it was probably ᶜAlī b. Mushir al-Kūfī[26] (d. 189/805) who originated it, because, although he was considered as *ṯiqa,* it is highly improbable that he could have met al-Musayyib al-Kūfī (d. 105/723), given that the temporal gap between them is rather wide. Lastly, in the *Tahḏīb,* under "al-Musayyib"[27] and "ᶜAlī b. Mushir,"[28] we do not find that they transmitted *ḥadīṯ*s from each other.

THE SUBCASE

A unique *ḥadīṯ* (*isnād* 33), considered as *ḥasan* and *ṣaḥīḥ* by al-Tirmiḏī,[29] concerns the subspecies of the succession of a daughter, one or more son's daughters and one or more full or consanguine sisters. A man went to Abū Mūsā al-Ašᶜarī al-Baṣrī[30] (d. 42/662–63) and Salmān b. Rabīᶜa al-Bāhilī[31] (d. 25/645–46), asking them about the solution of the case of a daughter, a son's daughter, and a full sister inheriting together. They answered: "One-half shall be due to the daughter and the remainder to the sister." But Ibn Masᶜūd said that he would have decided as the Messenger of Allāh did: one-half should be due to the daughter, one-sixth to the son's daughter to complete two-thirds, and the remainder to the sister.

Muṣannaf,[32] *Muṣannaf Ibn a. Šayba*[33] and *Ṣaḥīḥ Buḫārī*[34] have a short *matn;* they report only the statement of Ibn Masᶜūd about the decision of the Prophet. Only in *Muṣannaf Ibn a. Šayba* (no. 11125) does the *matn* end with the statement of Abū Bakr that "the estate shall be divided in six shares," which represents a strange and peculiar solution to the case given only by the transmitter Abū Ḫālid al-Aḥmar.

In *Frühislamisches, Musnad Ṭayālisī, Musnad Ibn Ḥanbal,*[35] *Ṣaḥīḥ Buḫārī,*[36] *Sunan Dāraquṭnī,*[37] and *Sunan Bayhaqī*[38] only Abū Mūsā is

---

[26] Cf. *Tahḏīb,* VII, 383–84, no. 623.
[27] See X, 153, no. 291.
[28] See VII, 383–84, no. 623.
[29] III, 281.
[30] *Riǧāl,* 23, no. 17; *Taḏkira,* I, 23–24, no. 10; *Tahḏīb,* V, 362–63, no. 625.
[31] *Tahḏīb,* IV, 136–37, no. 229.
[32] no. 19031.
[33] no. 11125.
[34] XXIII, 165.
[35] I, 428, 463–64.
[36] XXIII, 162.
[37] IV, 80, no. 41.
[38] VI, 229, 233.

mentioned. This leads us to suppose that the name of Salmān was added in the most recent works. Moreover, at the end of the *matn* in *Frühislamisches, Musnad Ṭayālisī, Musnad Ibn Ḥanbal,*[39] *Ṣaḥīḥ Buḫārī,* and *Sunan Bayhaqī* there is an addition: Abū Mūsā was informed about the statement of Ibn Masᶜūd and said "Do not ask me while this wise man is alive," which leads us to understand that there had been a change in the doctrine.

The scheme of the *matn* imitates *isnād*s 31 and 32. This is not an indication of its authenticity but apparently a literary device fashioned to give it credibility. It is quite simple: Abū Mūsā al-Ašᶜarī and Salmān b. Rabīᶜa exclude the son's daughter from the inheritance, applying literally the solution of Muᶜāḏ to the case; but a more ancient authority, Ibn Masᶜūd, relates a different solution from the Prophet. Thus, at the time of Abū Mūsā and Salmān, the doctrine was still uncertain, and it is unlikely in the extreme that the Prophet made such a decision about a subcase, giving that he said nothing about the main case.

The first transmitter is Huzayl;[40] the next is Abū Qays al-Kūfī (d. 120/737), the common transmitter, who did not have a high reputation among the Muslim critics.[41] Thus, we may infer that he probably was at the origin of the report.

To conclude, I believe that the doctrine regarding the main case goes back to the second half of the first century H., whether we consider the criterion of the common link (al-Aswad, d. 74/693–94) or we take into account the Iraqi and Medinese authorities supporting this doctrine. Every reference to the Prophet is fictitious, being the result of additions to the *matn.*

As far as the doctrine regarding the subcase is concerned, it was elaborated at the beginning of the second century H. at the time of Abū Qays (d. 120/737), the attempts to attribute it directly to the Prophet notwithstanding.

All law schools, after the initial denial on the part of the Meccan school, agreed on the doctrine of the *ᶜaṣaba maᶜa ġayrihi;* and all of

---

[39] I, 463–64.

[40] *Muḥallā* (IX, 256), *Muṣannaf Ibn a. Šayba* (XI, 245–46, nos. 11124–25), *Musnad Ṭayālisī* (49, no. 375), and *Šarḥ Nīl* (VIII, 295) have "Huḏayl." He was considered as *ṯiqa,* belonging to the first class (*ṭabaqa*) of the Kūfans (*Ṭabaqāt,* VI, 122; *Tahḏīb,* XI, 31, no. 69).

[41] The majority of them say that he is not consistent (*yuḫālif*) in his *ḥadīṯ*s, that he is not *ḥāfiẓ,* that his *ḥadīṯ* is not strong, but weak (*Ṭabaqāt,* VI, 225; *Tahḏīb,* VI, 152–53, no. 307).

them avoided committing injustice against full or consanguine sisters in favor of heirs who have a minor status in the Islamic law of inheritance.

CHAPTER FIVE

TAFSĪR LITERATURE AND JURIDICAL ELABORATION SUNNĪ, ZAYDĪ, ẒĀHIRĪ, AND IBĀḌĪ SCHOOLS

The traditions on *kalāla* do not contain a clear reference to the problem that was at the origin of the different interpretations of the term, even if they do provide some useful information. Why was there such a wide debate about its meaning? What are the questions involved? The answer appears clear if we consider that the different interpretations lead to different solutions regarding the position of the grandfather in the law of inheritance and the relations between daughters and full or consanguine sisters inheriting together. That the question of the definition of *kalāla* is connected with these two juridical questions emerges, on the one hand, from certain *ḥadīṯ*s[1] that also reveal that the entire mystery surrounding this term hides nothing more than an innovation on the Medinese part with respect to the previous agnatic doctrine. On the other hand, Mālik[2] clearly links the question of *kalāla* to that of the grandfather. Further, some of the *ḥadīṯ*s used to support the doctrine regarding the grandfather are the same, with some variations, as those on *kalāla.*[3] Lastly, the question of the *ᶜaṣaba maᶜa ġayrihi* is treated in the *tafsīr* of *Sūra* 4:176.[4] The grandfather is not a Qurᵓānic heir; so how could he be included among the heirs by quota? The means by which he could be included among the Qurᵓānic heirs was the reinterpretation of the term *kalāla.*[5] Does a daughter prevent a full or consanguine sister from inheritance? The issue was solved by reinterpreting the word *walad.* Thus the question was not merely a linguistic matter, but a truly legal issue. Real doctrines were in real opposition to each other.

---

[1] Cf. *isnād* 10 and *Aḥkām Qurᵓān,* I, 451.

[2] *Muwaṭṭaᵓ,* III, 113–15.

[3] The same *ḥadīṯ,* with the *isnād* ᶜUmar → Ṭāriq b. Šihāb → Qays b. Muslim → al-Aᶜmaš, is connected simultaneously with *kalāla* in *Tafsīr Ṭabarī* (IX, 439, no. 10882) and with the grandfather in *Sunan Bayhaqī* (VI, 245); the *matn* ends: "If Allāh had wanted to bring this affair to an end, He would certainly have done it," thus confirming ᶜUmar's ignorance of the answer.

[4] Cf., for instance, *Tafsīr Ṭabarī,* IX, 443–44.

[5] This research is thus complementary to that I carried out earlier on the position of the grandfather in the Islamic law of inheritance (cf. *Studies,* 1–32).

JURIDICAL SOURCES AND TAFSĪR *LITERATURE*

Many sources representing the various law schools do not deal with the definition of *kalāla.*[6] A few of them have some repeated but marginal information.[7] The Ẓāhirī works *Muḥallā* and *Marātib* contain conclusive information about the original meaning of the term and its transformation due to reinterpretation. Lastly, elaborate accounts can be found in *Kitāb al-Mabsūṭ* and *al-Muġnī.*

With reference to the *tafsīr* literature, I have examined chronologically the most important works, both Sunnī and Šīᶜī. As far as the Sunnī *tafsīr*s are concerned, nothing is said about *kalāla* in the *Tafsīr al-Qurʾān al-karīm* by the Kūfan Sufyān al-Ṯawrī[8] (d. 161/778). The richest source is surely the *Tafsīr al-Ṭabarī,* because it has much material and thoroughly discusses all the related issues, although it shows a clear tendency both to enrich the *matn*s and to quote certain new reports. Some information can be found in greater detail in the *Aḥkām al-Qurʾān* by Ibn al-ᶜArabī[9] (d. 543/1148) and in a very concise form in the *Tafsīr* of the Ḥanafī jurist and theologian al-Nasafī[10] (d. 710/1310).

The *tafsīr* of Faḫr al-Dīn al-Rāzī[11] (d. 606/1209), composed by al-Rāzī up to *Sūra* 8, and completed by his disciple Šams al-Dīn al-Ḫuwayyī (d. 637/1239), is of some interest. Although "al-Rāzī's zeal in the defense of Sunnism was always ardent and caused him to make many bitter enemies,"[12] in the particular case of the *tafsīr* of *Sūra* 4:12 and 4:176 he presents a hybrid of Sunnī and Šīᶜī doctrines. Indeed, on the one hand, he

---

[6] *Aḥkām, Āṯār, Corpus, Diritto, Farāʾiḍ, Fatāwā, Fiqh, Frühislamisches, Ǧāmiᶜ, Ǧāmiᶜ kabīr, Ḫizāna, Ḥuǧǧa, Ḫulāṣa, Iḥkām, Iḫtilāf Ṭaḥāwī, Kifāya, Masāʾil, Masāʾil Dāwūd, Minhāǧ, Mudawwana, Mudawwana kubrā, Muḫtaṣar Basīwī, Muḫtaṣar Ḫalīl, Muḫtaṣar Ḫiraqī, Muḫtaṣar Ibrāhīm, Muḫtaṣar Muzanī, Muḫtaṣar Qudūrī, Muḫtaṣar Ṭaḥāwī, Muqniᶜ, Muṣannaf Kindī, Muwaṭṭaʾ, Muwaṭṭaʾ Šaybānī, Nīl, Risāla Qayrawānī, Risāla Šāfiᶜī[1], Risāla Šāfiᶜī[2], Šarḥ Muwaṭṭaʾ Šaybānī, Šarḥ Siyar, Siyar, Sunna, Tuḥfa, ᶜUmda, Umm, Uṣūl, ᶜUyūn.* In *Muḫtaṣar Ḫalīl* (II, 821, no. 38) it is said only that the prevailing interpretation is that *kalāla* is a deceased person who has died leaving neither ascendants nor descendants, but the meaning of the term is disputed.

[7] *Baḥr, Ǧāmiᶜ Ibn Baraka, Kāfī, Šarḥ Muwaṭṭaʾ, Šarḥ Nīl.*

[8] He founded a short-lived legal *maḏhab* (*EI,* VII, 500–502; *GAS,* I, 518–19, no. 4).

[9] *EI²*, III, 707; *GAL,* S, I, 632–33, no. 5a.

[10] *EI²*, VII, 969; *GAL,* II, 250–53; S, II, 263–68.

[11] *EI²*, II, 751–55; *GAS,* I, 666–69, no. 6; S, I, 920–24, no. 6.

[12] *EI²*, II, 752.

attributes the well-known definition of *kalāla* that makes reference to *wālid* and *walad* to Abū Bakr,[13] but fails here to follow the Šīʿī doctrine on the *ʿaṣaba maʿa ġayrihi.*[14] On the other hand, he also attributes the Šīʿī definition of *kalāla* as referring to *wālidān* and *walad* to Abū Bakr.[15] Surely there is a contradiction in his discussion, because one can hardly harmonize the Sunnī and Šīʿī systems of inheritance.[16] The influence of the Šīʿī doctrine appears completely when al-Rāzī writes that there is no doubt that brothers/sisters are prevented from inheritance by the presence of the parents (*wālidān*), because the deceased is not *kalāla* if parents are present.[17]

Another very interesting commentary is the *tafsīr* by al-Niẓām al-Nīsābūrī.[18] He lived during the ninth century H., and he was alive in the middle of that century.[19] Whether he was Sunnī or Šīʿī is controversial. *GAL* says nothing on the matter, but simply includes him under the rubric *Die Qorʾānwissenschaften.* According to the author of the *Aʿyān*[20] *tašayyuʿ* does not seem to appear in his *tafsīr,* whereas others say that some evidence of *Šīʿa* loyalties is to be found there. In reality, al-Nīsābūrī followed the *maḏhab* of *ahl al-Sunna waʾl-ǧamāʿa* and he expounded their *uṣūl;* but for the *furūʿ* he mentioned every denomination (*ṭāʾifa*) without any fanaticism (*taʿaṣṣub*) or quarrel (*mirāʾ*).[21] This becomes clear in the context of the commentary on *Sūra* 4:12 and 4:176. As a matter of fact, Nīsābūrī reports in his *Tafsīr* the well-known *ḥadīṯ* material and his reasoning is similar to that of the Sunnīs, although he introduces specifically Šīʿī doctrines as well. There is a close and evident relationship between *Tafsīr Rāzī* and *Tafsīr Nīsābūrī,* both with reference to content and to form. This link appears also in the acceptance of the Sunnī doctrine of the *ʿaṣaba maʿa ġayrihi* in *Tafsīr Nīsābūrī,*[22] in the same manner as in *Tafsīr Rāzī.* Both texts indiscriminately gather opposing doctrines; the knowledge of their origin may have been forgotten.

---

[13] *Tafsīr Rāzī,* II, 378.

[14] Ibid., 575.

[15] Ibid., 378.

[16] Cf. *Dir. ered. I; Dir ered. II.*

[17] *Tafsīr Rāzī,* II, 379.

[18] *Aʿyān,* XXIII, 112–15, no. 4514; *GAL,* II, 256, no. 2; *GAL,* S, II, 273, no. 2a.

[19] *GAL* (II, 256, no. 2; S, II, 273, no. 2a) wrongly writes "c. VIII H."

[20] XXIII, 113.

[21] *Aʿyān,* XXIII, 114.

[22] VI, 35–36.

In modern times, one of the most important Sunnī commentaries is the *Tafsīr al-Manār* by Muḥammad ᶜAbduh[23] (d. 1323/1905) and Muḥammad Rašīd Riḍā[24] (d. 1354/1935). The commentary includes the contributions of Muḥammad ᶜAbduh up to *Sūra* 4:125, whereas Rašīd Riḍā continued to the end of *Sūra* 12.[25] This *tafsīr* uncritically reproduces much of the material contained in previous works. In particular, it relates both the definitions of *kalāla* (referring to *wālid* and *walad*[26] and to *awlād* and *wālidān*); and *kalāla* is presented both as a quality of the deceased and of the heirs.[27] A certain influence of al-Rāzī, the only author quoted in this context, is evident in the *Tafsīr al-Manār.* [28]

As for the Šīᶜī commentaries on the Qurᵓān, the *tafsīr* by Furāt al-Kūfī[29] (d. ca. 310/922) contains nothing on *kalāla* in *Sūrat al-nisāᵓ*,[30] because the main intent of the author was to gather what had been revealed about *ahl al-Bayt.* However al-Ṭūsī (d. 460/1067), in *al-Tibyān fī tafsīr al-Qurᵓān,* includes the materials on *kalāla,* following a reasoning, however, similar to that of the Sunnīs.[31] Then, in a separate section, he discusses the Imāmī doctrine on inheritance independently.[32] Lastly, *Mağmaᶜ al-Bayān fī tafsīr al-Qurᵓān* by al-Ṭabarsī[33] (d. 548/1153) is dependent on *Tafsīr Ṭūsī,* and follows the same scheme: first it examines the well known materials,[34] and then it briefly discusses the Imāmī law of inheritance.[35] For this reason, both of these works have been examined in the context of the Sunnī elaboration of *kalāla.*

Two points are relevant here. First, the Imāmī definition of *kalāla* (with its characteristic reference to *wālidān* and *walad*) does not appear in *Tafsīr Ṭūsī* and *Mağmaᶜ;* only *wālid* and *walad* are mentioned (Abū Bakr's definition). Secondly, the Šīᶜī materials found in the Šīᶜī collections of traditions were never used in the Imāmī *tafsīr*s, not even in the

---

23 *EI²*, VII, 418–20; *GAL,* III, 315–21, no. 2.

24 *EI²*, VIII, 446–48; *GAL,* III, 321–23, no. 3.

25 *EI²*, VI, 361.

26 *Tafsīr Manār,* IV, 422; VI, 105, 106, 107, 108.

27 Ibid., 422–23.

28 Ibid., IV, 422.

29 *GAS,* I, 539, no. 32.

30 *Tafsīr Furāt,* I, 101–16.

31 *Tafsīr Ṭūsī,* III, 135–37.

32 Ibid., 137–39.

33 *GAL,* I, 513–14, no. 3; S, I, 708–9, no. 3.

34 *Mağmaᶜ*, II, 16–17.

35 Ibid., 18.

tafsīr of al-Ṭūsī, who himself wrote some works devoted exclusively to the gathering of Imāmī traditions.

TAFSĪR *LITERATURE:* SŪRA *4:12*

The generally accepted reading given by Saᶜd b. Abī Waqqāṣ (d. 51/671),[36] also attributed to ᶜAbd Allāh b. Masᶜūd, is well known:[37] ". . . and he has a [uterine] brother or a [uterine] sister. . . ." This Qurʾānic verse raises, however, particular questions, which are the reading of the root *w-r-ṯ*, and, consequently, who *kalāla* is in that context; and, then, why *kalāla* is in the accusative case.

1. READING OF THE VERBAL FORM *Y-W-R-Ṯ*

The *qurrāʾ* diverged on the reading of this verse. Thus the verbal form *y-w-r-ṯ* was read in context as *wa-in kāna rağul^un* yūraṯu *kalālat^an*,[38] deriving *yūraṯu* from the passive verb *wuriṯa/yūraṯu,* not from the active, transitive verb *awraṯa/yūriṯu.* The alternative reading, attributed to al-Ḥasan, was *yūriṯu.*[39] A third, but not a very much followed, reading was *yuwarriṯu.*[40]

2. WHO IS *KALĀLA*?

The reading of *Sūra* 4:12 and the attribution of the term *kalāla* are connected. The first question is linked to the second one, which is a direct consequence of the first. Depending on which of the first two variant readings is followed, the attribution of *kalāla* changes; however, this dif-

---

[36] *Dir. ered. II,* 215, n. 1; *Ḫilāf,* II, 263, *masʾala* 26; *Kāfī,* II, 536; *Mabsūṭ,* XXIX, 151; *Muġnī,* VII, 4; *Muṣannaf Ibn a. Šayba,* XI, 416–17, no. 11650; *Musnad Dārimī,* II, 264, no. 2979; *Šarḥ Muwaṭṭaʾ,* III, 105; *Tafsīr Manār,* IV, 424; *Tafsīr Nīsābūrī,* IV, 201; *Tafsīr Rāzī,* II, 379–80; *Tafsīr Ṭabarī,* VIII, 61–62, nos. 8772–75. This is also the interpretation of Qatāda al-Baṣrī (d. 117/735) (*Tafsīr Ṭabarī,* VIII, 62, no. 8776) and al-Suddī al-Kūfī (d. 127/744–45) (*Tafsīr Ṭabarī,* VIII, 62–63, no. 8778). On Saᶜd b. Abī Waqqāṣ, who embraced Islam at a very early date (*qadīm^an*), see *Tahḏīb,* III, 483–84, no. 901. The interpretation was likewise that of ᶜAṭiyya b. Saᶜd al-ᶜAwfī al-Kūfī (d. 111/729) (*Baḥr,* V, 339), who was counted among the Šīᶜa of *ahl al-Kūfa* but considered as weak (*ḍaᶜīf*) (see *Aᶜlām,* V, 32; *GAS,* I, 30–31, no. 6; *Ṭabaqāt,* VI, 212–13; *Tahḏīb,* VII, 224–26, no. 413). *Baḥr* (V, 339) relates a strange doctrine, attributed to ᶜUbayd b. ᶜUmayr, according to which in Qurʾān 4:12 it is consanguine brothers that are referred to.

[37] *Ḫilāf,* II, 263, *masʾala* 26; *Kāfī,* II, 536; *Šarḥ Muwaṭṭaʾ,* III, 106.

[38] *Aḥkām Qurʾān,* I, 447; *Lisān,* XI, 592; *Tahḏīb luġa,* IX, 447–48.

[39] *Aḥkām Qurʾān,* I, 447, 448; *Lisān,* XI, 594; *Mağmaᶜ,* II, 16, 149.

[40] *Aḥkām Qurʾān,* I, 447, 48.

ference has no consequence for the legal doctrine since the juridical rules remain the same in both cases. Moreover, one must consider that in Arabic some other words refer indifferently to two complementary referents; e.g., *mawlā* (master/client), *ġarīm* (creditor/debtor), *ḥaqq* (right/duty). What is remarkable here is that some scholars report indifferently the Sunnī as well as the Šīᶜī definition of *kalāla,* ignoring their doctrinal implications.

a) Wa-in kāna rağul^{un} yūraṯu kalālat^{an}: kalāla *a quality of the deceased*

The reading *yūraṯu* has as a consequence that *kalāla* must refer to the deceased if he leaves his inheritance to heirs other than *walad* or *wālid.* According to the different etymology of the term, those who derive it from *kalla/yakillu* believe, as Ibn Barrī al-Miṣrī[41] (d. 582/1187) said, that *kalāla* was originally a quality of the deceased: a deceased person becomes feeble if he has died leaving neither *walad* nor *wālid* as heirs. Based on this etymology, the Sunnī al-Rāzī[42] infers that the weakness in the relation implies that two relatives are not linked with each other directly, but through another relative (*bi-wāsiṭat al-ġayr*). Moreover *Tafsīr Nīsābūrī*[43] holds that the most authentic statement is that of Abū Bakr, because *kalāla,* in its origin (*fī ᵓl-aṣl*), is an infinitive with the same meaning as *kalāl;* that is, the falling away of vigor, as is confirmed in a verse by the poet al-Aᶜšā Maymūn b. Qays.[44] Thus the *kalāla* is the deceased. *Tafsīr Manār* shares this opinion.[45] However, strangely enough, *Tafsīr Nīsābūrī* and *Tafsīr Manār,* although they are Sunnī sources (with some doubts as to *Tafsīr Nīsābūrī*), relate the Šīᶜī definition of *kalāla* as a person having neither *awlād* nor *wālidān.*

The attribution of *kalāla* to the deceased is founded on three *ḥadīṯs*[46] in which it is said: "A *kalāla* is a person who. . . ."[47] Moreover, Ibn Abī Šayba[48] (alone) relates a very dubious *ḥadīṯ,* with an incomplete *isnād,* the *matn* of which is simply "Ibn ᶜAbbās said: *al-kalāla huwa ᵓl-mayyit.*"[49]

---

[41] *Lisān,* XI, 593; *Tāğ,* VIII, 101.

[42] *Tafsīr Rāzī,* II, 378.

[43] IV, 201; VI, 35.

[44] See chapter one.

[45] IV, 422–23.

[46] *isnād*s 5, 18, and 21.

[47] *Tafsīr Ṭabarī,* VIII, 58.

[48] *Muṣannaf Ibn a. Šayba,* XI, 417, no. 11653.

[49] The verse of al-Farazdaq discussed in chapter one also supports this view by stressing that the Umayyads did not inherit kingship from collaterals, but

This is the doctrine followed by *ahl al-Baṣra,* among whom al-Saraḫsī[50] mentions Abū ᶜUbayda al-Baṣrī. The proof is the *tafsīr* of Qurᵓān 4:12 that states: "If a man or woman, dying, leaves his/her inheritance as *kalāla."* As only a deceased person can leave an inheritance, *kalāla* is *ḥāl* and it is a quality of a deceased person.[51] The Zaydī work *Baḥr*[52] says that this is the belief of the majority of the Companions and of al-Suddī.

b) Wa-in kāna rağulᵘⁿ yūriṯu kalālatᵃⁿ: kalāla *a quality of the heirs*

The alternative reading *yūriṯu* means that *kalāla* are the heirs, that is, the uterine brothers/sisters. Those who derive *kalāla* from *takallala,* believe that it would mean: a man leaves his inheritance to collateral kin, as if he wore a crown.[53] This means: if a person, dying, leaves an inheritance to those who surround him as a crown; that is to say, a brother or a sister who surrounds him by his or her kinship.[54] Thus, *kalāla* are the heirs, be they brothers, sisters, or others, when there is neither *walad* nor *wālid.*[55] Based on this etymology, the Sunnī al-Rāzī[56] infers that *kalāla* cannot refer to the *walad* and the *wālidān,* but only to collaterals, as the Imāmīs and the Ismāᶜīlīs say. *Ahl al-Kūfa, ahl al-Madīna,* and the Ḥiğāzīs follow this doctrine; and their proof is Qurᵓān 4:176: "They will ask thee for a legal decision. . . ." So, it seems correct that one is asked only about heirs, in this case about those heirs among whom there is neither *walad* nor *wālid.*[57]

---

through a direct line. *Tafsīr Nīsābūrī,* IV, 201; *Tafsīr Rāzī,* II, 379.

[50] *Mabsūṭ,* XXIX, 153.

[51] *Ḫilāf,* II, 263; *Lisān,* XI, 593, 594; *Mabsūṭ,* XXIX, 153; *Tāğ,* VIII, 101.

[52] V, 339.

[53] *Aḥkām Qurᵓān,* I, 447, 448; *Durr,* IV, 31; *Kāfī,* II, 538; *Mabsūṭ,* XXIX, 153; *Mağmaᶜ,* II, 17; *Tafsīr Nasafī,* I, 212; *Tafsīr Ṭabarī,* VIII, 53; *Tafsīr Ṭūsī,* III, 135. *Muġnī* (VII, 5) writes that it was related thus from ᶜUmar, ᶜAlī, Ibn Masᶜūd, and al-Zuhrī.

[54] *Lisān,* XI, 592; *Mabsūṭ,* XXIX, 153; *Tafsīr Ṭabarī,* VIII, 53.

[55] *Durr,* IV, 31; *Kāfī,* II, 538; *Mağmaᶜ,* II, 17, 149; *Muġnī,* VII, 5; *Nihāya,* IV, 31; *Šarḥ Nīl,* VIII, 298–99; *Tafsīr Nasafī,* I, 212; *Tafsīr Nīsābūrī,* IV, 201; VI, 35; *Tafsīr Ṭabarī,* VIII, 60; *Tafsīr Ṭūsī,* III, 135. However, al-Ṭūsī misunderstands the statement, because he takes *kalāla* to refer also to husband and wife, who are obviously heirs, but not relatives on a collateral line. *Tafsīr Manār* (IV, 423) writes that it is the heirs except *awlād* and *wālidān;* thus reflecting the Ismāᶜīlī and Imāmī doctrine.

[56] *Tafsīr Rāzī,* II, 378–79.

[57] *Ḫilāf,* II, 263; *Lisān,* XI, 594; *Mabsūṭ,* XXIX, 153.

Besides the last verse of *Sūrat al-nisāʾ,* which supports this view of *kalāla* as a quality of the heirs, the attribution is founded only on certain other religious arguments. Thus al-Ṭabarī[58] believes that *kalāla* are those who inherit from the deceased in the absence of *walad* and *wālid.* He bases his statement on a *ḫabar* from Ǧābir b. ᶜAbd Allāh, who at the time in which the report is placed had neither *walad* nor *wālid,*[59] and on two other *ḥadīṯ*s[60] containing this sentence: "I have no other heir than *kalāla.*" In the same vein the traditionist and jurist al-Sāǧī al-Baṣrī[61] (d. 307/920) stated: "This is what the linguists have said."[62]

The Zaydī work *Baḥr*[63] reports that this view of *kalāla* is the stated opinion of some of the Companions and of Saᶜīd b. Ǧubayr al-Kūfī[64] (d. 95/714). However there was much confusion regarding this question among the Muslim jurists. As a matter of fact, the Ḥanafī jurist al-Saraḫsī indiscriminately qualifies both the deceased and the heirs as *kalāla* in two different places dealing with uterine brothers (*al-kalāla man laysa lahu walad wa-wālid;*[65] *al-kalāla mā ḫalā ʾl-wālid waʾl-walad*).[66] Then the Sunnī al-Rāzī,[67] following the Ismāᶜīlī and Imāmī doctrine, interprets the term in Qurʾān 4:176 as a deceased person leaving neither *wālidān* (both parents) nor *walad.* However, in other places, he arbitrarily refers both to the deceased and to the heirs as *kalāla:* if *kalāla* is considered a quality of the heir, it is understood as those heirs except *awlād* (children, offspring) and *wālidān;* if, instead, it is taken to refer to the deceased, it means a person without *awlād* and *wālidān.*[68]

The position of Ibn Qudāma is likewise uncertain. In fact, with reference to the full or consanguine brothers of Qurʾān 4:176, he states: *al-kalāla man lā walad lahu wa-lā wālid;*[69] and the same definition is re-

---

58 *Tafsīr Ṭabarī,* VIII, 60.

59 *Lisān,* XI, 592, 594; *Maǧmaᶜ,* II, 17, 149; *Muġnī,* VII, 5; *Tafsīr Nīsābūrī,* IV, 201; *Tafsīr Rāzī,* II, 379; *Tafsīr Ṭabarī,* VIII, 33, no. 8730; *Tahḏīb luġa,* IX, 447, 448.

60 *Tafsīr Ṭabarī,* VIII, 60–61, nos. 8770–71.

61 *GAS,* I, 349–50, no. 4.

62 *Ḫilāf,* II, 263.

63 V, 339.

64 *Aᶜlām,* III, 145; *Ḥuffāẓ,* 31, no. 71; *Riǧāl Kaššī,* 110, no. 55; *Ṭabaqāt,* VI, 178–87; *Taḏkira,* I, 76–77.

65 *Mabsūṭ,* XXIX, 146.

66 Ibid., 154.

67 *Tafsīr Rāzī,* II, 379.

68 Ibid., 378, 379, 575.

69 *Muġnī,* VII, 3.

peated for the uterine brothers of Qurʾān 4:12,[70] with the addition *fī qawl al-ǧumhūr* (according to the generally accepted opinion); thus *kalāla* is the deceased. Ibn Qudāma seems to follow the same view in *Kāfī,*[71] at least with regard to Qurʾān 4:12. But in *Muġnī* later on,[72] explaining the doctrine of those who consider a grandfather to have the same legal status as a father, not only does he attribute the term *kalāla* to the heirs (*al-kalāla ism*^un^ *liʾl-wāriṯ maᶜa ᶜadam al-walad waʾl-wālid*), but he also gives the definition proper to the Ismāᶜīlī and Imāmī schools, although without quoting them: *kalāla* are the heirs except *al-wālidān* and *al-mawlūdūn* (children).[73] What is more surprising is that Ibn Qudāma maintains that Ibn Ḥanbal stipulated (*naṣṣa*) this. Generally speaking, Aḥmad's juridical doctrine is uncertain; furthermore, in this case such an attribution is quite improbable because it is contrary to what he maintained about the succession of any brothers/sisters inheriting together with a grandfather. Moreover, *Kāfī,*[74] which reflects the *fiqh* of Aḥmad, does not attribute any definition of *kalāla* to him.

Lastly, the Ibāḍī jurist Ibn Baraka[75] is inclined to believe that *kalāla* is a quality of the heir, while another Ibāḍī text, *Šarḥ Nīl,*[76] maintains that it describes the deceased.

c) Kalāla *is both the deceased and the heirs*

A third opinion ascribes the quality of *kalāla* both to the deceased and to the heirs. However, it is based only on a single *ḥadīṯ,*[77] known only to al-Ṭabarī, and related only on the authority of Ibn Zayd, an obscure traditionist.[78] This doctrine was also maintained by al-Wāḥidī[79] (d. 468/1075), in his *Tafsīr;* in fact, according to him, one can say "the person who has died having neither *walad* nor *wālid* is the *kalāla* of his heirs," and "the heirs among whom there is neither *walad* nor *wālid* are the *kalāla* of the deceased."[80]

---

[70] Ibid., 4.
[71] II, 538.
[72] VII, 66.
[73] Ibid., 5.
[74] II, 538.
[75] *Ǧāmiᶜ Ibn Baraka,* II, 594. He gives the definition of *kalāla* as the heirs with the exclusion of father and son (. . . *al-kalāla, fa-mā dūna ʾl-ab waʾl-ibn*) (ibid., 570). The *ǧadd* is not among the *kalāla* (ibid., 594).
[76] VIII, 298.
[77] *isnād* 6.
[78] *Tafsīr Ṭabarī,* VIII, 60. See also *Nihāya,* IV, 31.
[79] *GAL,* I, 524, no. 3; S, I, 730–31, no. 4; *Iršād,* V, 97–102, no. 41.
[80] *Šarḥ Nīl,* VIII, 299.

d) Kalāla *is maternal kinship*

Another view, which seems to be nothing but a personal inference based on the verse by al-Farazdaq, related anonymously by Ibn Qudāma,[81] was that *kalāla* is maternal kinship (*qarābat al-umm*). Ibn Qudāma, as noted above, understood "You inherited the scepter of kingship, not as collaterals (*ġayr^a kalālat^in*)" in the verse to mean "you inherited the kingship from your paternal ancestors (*ābāʾ*), not from your maternal ascendants (*ummahāt*)."[82]

e) Kalāla *is the estate*

Lastly, an isolated and unfounded doctrine is asserted by the Baṣran philologist al-Naḍr b. Šumayl[83] (d. 203/878), a man learned in the *ayyām al-ʿArab, ḥadīṯ,* and *fiqh al-luġa,* who wrote a work on *ġarīb al-ḥadīṯ.* He maintained that *kalāla* is the estate (*māl*).[84]

3. THE WORD GOVERNING THE ACCUSATIVE CASE OF *KALĀLA*

The elaboration of this question, involving Qurʾān 4:12 exclusively, is not very ancient, and it is treated only in some sources.

If kalāla *is a quality of the deceased*

The most obvious justifications of the accusative case are if we refer *kalāla* to the deceased. In al-Ṭabarī (d. 310/923) two alternative interpretations are proposed: a) *kalāla* is in the accusative because it is *ḫabar kāna,* while the verb *yūraṯu* is considered as *ṣifa* of the word *rağul^un*: "If a man, who is inherited from, is *kalāla";* b) *kāna* is considered as a verb that has no need of a *ḫabar,* like the verb *waqaʿa;* the accusative of *kalāla* being then considered as *ḥāl,* that is, "he is inherited from being *kalāla,"* as one may say "he is being beaten while standing (*yuḍrabu qāʾim^an*)."[85]

---

[81] *Muġnī,* VII, 5.

[82] According to a statement related in some linguistic sources (*Ğamhara,* I, 120; *Lisān,* XI, 592; *Muḥkam,* VI, 410; *Qāmūs,* IV, 45; *Tāğ,* VIII, 101), *kalāla* are the uterine brothers/sisters.

[83] *Aʿlām,* VIII, 357–58; *GAL,* I, 101, no. 7; S, I, 161, no. 7; *GAS,* 262; *Tahḏīb,* X, 437–38, no. 795.

[84] *Baḥr,* V, 339. Anonymously quoted in *Aḥkām Qurʾān,* I, 449, 451.

[85] *Tafsīr Ṭabarī,* VIII, 58. The opinion is repeated in *Mağmaʿ,* II, 17; *Šarḥ Muwaṭṭaʾ,* III, 105, 106; *Tafsīr Nīsābūrī,* IV, 201; *Tafsīr Ṭūsī,* III, 135. *Tafsīr Nasafī* (I, 212) relates the accusative only as *ḫabar kāna. Aḥkām Qurʾān* (I, 447) and *Šarḥ Nīl* (VIII, 298) relate the accusative only as *ḥāl.* Al-Azharī (d. 370/980) (*Tahḏīb luġa,* IX, 448; repeated in *Lisān,* XI, 592) accepted only the hypothesis that *kalāla* is in the accusative case as *ḥāl.* The meaning of the

Al-Ṭabarī gives a third explanation of his own.[86] He believes, as outlined above, that it is right that *kalāla* is in the accusative because of the verb *yūraṯu,* while *yūraṯu* is *ḫabar kāna.* However, according to al-Ṭabarī, even if *kalāla* is in the accusative depending on *yūraṯu,* it is not in the accusative as *ḥāl,* but because it is an infinitive, as if the sentence were: *wa-in kāna rağul^un yūraṯu [mutakallilahu ʾl-nasab] kalālat^an* ("If a man, [dying], is inherited from [crowned by kinship] because of his being *kalāla*"). In other words, *kalālat^an* (infinitive of *kalla*) is to be considered as a *mafʿūl lahu.* Thus this explanation, like the two preceding ones, presumes that *kalāla* is the deceased.

The most extensive justification of the accusative case of *kalāla,* which parallels the points made by al-Ṭabarī, is in *Tafsīr Rāzī*[87] and in *Lisān al-ʿArab,*[88] where a further distinction is made. If the verb is *wariṯa/yariṯu,* in the passive form, *kalāla* thus being taken as a quality of the deceased, two solutions given by the Baṣrans are important: *kalāla* is the *ḫabar* (predicate) of *kāna* ("if he [the deceased] is *kalāla,* i.e., feeble, having neither *walad* nor *wālid*"), *or* it is *ḥāl* (adverb of state) modifying *yūraṯu* ("if he is inherited from while he is *kalāla*"). The verb *kāna,* in this second case, is considered complete (*tāmma*), having no need of a *ḫabar.* It is not correct, according to this view, that *kāna* is defective (*nāqiṣa*), as the Egyptian grammarian, lexicographer, and commentator of the Qurʾān, al-Ḥawfī[89] (d. 430/1039), said. If *kāna* were *nāqiṣa,* the only available *ḫabar* would be *kalāla.* Since this word refers to the *mawrūṯ* anyway, the addition of *yūraṯu* would be superfluous; i.e., "if a man is inherited from while he is *kalāla,* that is, feeble."[90] Moreover, a third justification is possible: *kalāla* (as infinitive of *kalla*) is in the accusative because it is *mafʿūl lahu;* that is: "He is inherited from because he is *kalāla.*"[91]

If kalāla *is a quality of the heirs*

The accusative case of *kalāla* is more complicated to explain when the

---

Qurʾānic verse is, then, a person has died in the condition (status, *ḥāl*) where he is surrounded by the kinship of his heirs, i.e., he has neither *wālid* nor *walad,* but a uterine brother/sister.

[86] *Tafsīr Ṭabarī,* VIII, 58. *Tafsīr Nasafī* (I, 212) repeats this doctrine; but it is said that *yūraṯu* is *ḫabar kāna,* and that *kalāla* is *ḥāl* depending on *yūraṯu.*

[87] II, 379.

[88] XI, 593. Almost completely repeated in *Tāğ al-ʿarūs,* VIII, 101–2.

[89] *GAL,* I, 523, no. 1; S, I, 729, no. 2; *GAS,* VIII, 246–47.

[90] *Lisān,* XI, 593; *Tafsīr Rāzī,* II, 379; *Tāğ,* VIII, 101.

[91] *Tafsīr Nīsābūrī,* IV, 201; *Tafsīr Rāzī,* II, 379.

word is considered as a quality of the heirs, the verb accordingly being presumed to be in its fourth form, *awraṯa/yūriṯu*. This difficulty suggests that the original and most normal attribution of *kalāla* is to the deceased. In fact, when *kalāla* is conceived of as applying to the heirs, it is assumed that some part of the sentence is elided. The justifications given in *Lisān al-ᶜArab* are three:[92]

1) *Kalāla* is an infinitive, it being assumed that the first member of the construct (*muḍāf*) is elided: "He dies leaving his inheritance [as a bequest to] remote kin (*yūraṯu [wirāṯatᵃ] kalālatⁱⁿ*)," as the verse by al-Farazdaq implies; that is, you inherited it (kingship) as the inheritance from a close relative, not as the inheritance from a remote one. The verse by ᶜĀmir b. al-Ṭufayl suggests the same: "It was not for my kinsmen's sake that ᶜĀmir made me their chief." Because of this, one can say: "He is a remote paternal cousin by a remote relationship (*huwa ibn ᶜammⁱⁿ kalālatᵃⁿ*)," that is, by a remote kinship (*baᶜīd al-nasab*). If one refers to close kinship (*al-qurb*), he says: "He is a close paternal cousin by a close kinship (*huwa ibn ᶜammⁱⁿ dinyatᵃⁿ*)."[93]

2) *Kalāla* is an infinitive in the adverbial function of a *ḥāl,* as when one says: "Zayd came running (using *rakḍᵃⁿ* for *rākiḍᵃⁿ*)"; "He is my paternal cousin because of his being a close relative (using *dinyatᵃⁿ* for *dāniyᵃⁿ*)"; "He is my paternal cousin because of his being remote in his kinship (*kalālatᵃⁿ;* i.e., *baᶜīdᵃⁿ fī ᵓl-nasab*)." In this case, one must consider *kalāla* as a *ḥāl* with a pronoun (*ḍamīr*) connected with the verb *yūriṯu,* that is, *ḏā kalālatⁱⁿ:* "He dies leaving an inheritance, as one having remote kin."[94]

3) Al-Ṭabarī[95] relates that some anonymous Baṣrans said: *"Kalāla* is *ḫabar kāna;* however, *kalāla* is not the deceased, but the heir." This view is better discussed in *Lisān al-ᶜArab* and it is repeated in *Tāǧ al-ᶜarūs. Kalāla* is *ḫabar kāna,* the first member of the construct state (*muḍāf*) being presumed to be elided: "when a deceased person has a remote relation (*ḏā kalālatⁱⁿ*)." Further on the *Lisān* specifies, "If a man, who, dying, leaves as an heir (makes inherit, *yūriṯu*) a remote relation (*ḏā kalālatⁱⁿ*)," one can say that he has a *ḏā qarābatⁱⁿ,* among them (the heirs) there being neither *walad* nor *wālid."*[96]

---

[92] *Tafsīr Nīsābūrī* (IV, 201) and *Tafsīr Rāzī* (II, 379) say that the accusative is justified in the same three ways examined here.

[93] *Lisān,* XI, 593–94.

[94] *Lisān,* XI, 594; *Tāǧ,* VIII, 102.

[95] *Tafsīr Ṭabarī,* VIII, 58.

[96] *Lisān,* XI, 594; *Tāǧ,* VIII, 102.

With reference to the reading *yūriṯu kalālat^an* and *yuwarriṯu kalālat^an*, the statement of ᶜUṯmān b. Ğinnī al-Mawṣilī[97] (d. 392/1002) is noteworthy. He believes that two objects of *yūriṯu* or *yuwarriṯu* are elided, i.e., *yūriṯu [wāriṯahu mālahu]:* "A man, who, dying, bequeaths [his estate to his heir], is *kalāla."* Ibn Ğinnī remarks that, in such a way, *kalāla* is in the accusative because it is *ḫabar kāna* or a *maṣdar,* so that *kalāla* is a quality of the deceased, not of the heir. But, according to Ibn Ğinnī, it seems that *kalāla* is an infinitive referring to the heir as well as to the deceased; in fact, a *maṣdar* may refer sometimes to the subject and sometimes to the object.[98]

SUNNĪ, ZAYDĪ, ẒĀHIRĪ, AND IBĀḌĪ SCHOOLS

The three previously examined questions do not touch the real core of the problem, which regards the interpretation of the definitions of the word *kalāla* found in the *ḥadīṯ* literature. In brief, the juridical elaboration was as follows.

As regards maternal half-siblings:

kalāla = person who has died leaving neither *walad* nor *wālid* (forefathers) (*man lā walad lahu wa-lā wālid*) (all the schools)
walad = male descendants of any degree, and daughters and female descendants of male children of any degree (all the schools)
wālid = father and true grandfather (all the schools)

Regarding full or consanguine siblings:

kalāla = person who has died leaving neither *walad* nor *wālid* (Ḥanafīs, Ẓāhirīs, Ibāḍīs); person who has died leaving neither *walad* nor *ab* (father) (Mālikīs, Šāfiᶜīs, Ḥanbalīs, Zaydīs)
walad = a) male descendants of any degree alone or together with daughters or female descendants of male children of any degree, brothers/sisters being thereby excluded from inheritance (all the schools); b) male descendants of any degree alone—one sister or more cannot inherit as *ᶜaṣaba maᶜa ġayrihi* together with one daughter or more (Sunnīs, Zaydīs, Ibāḍīs); c) daughters or son's daughters, sisters being considered as *ᶜaṣaba* only if there is not any other *ᶜāṣib bi-nafsihi* (Ẓāhirīs)
wālid = father, true grandfather (Ḥanafīs, Ẓāhirīs, Ibāḍīs)

---

[97] *Aᶜlām,* IV, 364; *EI²,* III, 754; *GAL,* I, 131, no. 10; S, I, 191–93, no. 10; *GAS,* VIII, 15, 142, 255; IX, 173–82; *Iršād,* V, 15–32.

[98] *Lisān,* XI, 594; *Tāğ,* VIII, 102.

From this scheme it appears that, apart from the definition of *kalāla* appropriate to each school and adapted to its own purposes, what created a problem was the meaning of *walad* and *wālid.*

Of the two Qur°ānic verses involved, only the second (Qur°ān 4:176) presented problems in its purport,[99] whereas there were no divergences on Qur°ān 4:12. Indeed, the Sunnī as well as the Zaydī, Ẓāhirī, and Ibāḍī schools believe that uterine brothers and/or sisters are prevented from inheritance by direct descendants, by the sons' descendants, however low, be they males or females, by the father, and by a true grandfather, or any other ascendant in a male line.[100] Thus, in this context *kalāla* means a person who has died leaving neither ascendants nor descendants (*al-kalāla man lam yatruk walad^an wa-lā wālid^an*), as a *matn* attributed to Ibn ᶜAbbās says,[101] and as another *matn,* attributed to Qatāda, specifies: *lā ab wa-lā ğadd wa-lā ibn wa-lā ibna.*[102] Therefore, *wālid* means father or any other male ascendant, while *walad* means sons and daughters or any other male, as well as female, descendants.[103] The Zaydī jurist Ibn al-Murtaḍā[104] formulated this doctrine as follows: *al-kalāla man lā walad lahu wa-lā wālid wa-lā ğadd.* How is it that this interpretation can be right with reference to *Sūra* 4:12, while it is not appropriate with reference to *Sūra* 4:176? The question is not merely of academic or

[99] *Mabsūṭ* (XXIX, 151) states with respect to Qur°ān 4:12 that the mode of expression is very obscure (*mubham ğidd^an*) compared to Qur°ān 4:176, where at least the word *walad* appears. However, I believe that this difficulty is due not to the purport of these verses, but, above all, to their reading, the etymology of the word *kalāla,* and the juridical doctrines implied in both verses.

[100] *Dir. ered. II,* 216.

[101] *Tafsīr Ṭabarī,* VIII, 56, no. 8755.

[102] *Tafsīr Ṭabarī,* VIII, 57, no. 8760. This definition is also attributed to Ibn ᶜAbbās: *"Kalāla* is a person who has died leaving no *walad."* This is because he makes the uterine brothers inherit a one-sixth of the estate together with the parents of the deceased (*abawān*) (*Tafsīr Ṭabarī,* VIII, 57), according to a *ḥadīṯ* on his authority (with the *isnād:* Ṭāwūs → Ibn Ṭāwūs → Maᶜmar) that states that the portion of the estate subtracted from the share of the mother because of the presence of two or more uterine brothers shall be due to them (*Tafsīr Ṭabarī,* VIII, 45, no. 8734). But al-Ṭabarī (VIII, 45), referring to *isnād* 21, adds that a different opinion is known from Ibn ᶜAbbās.

[103] *Lisān,* III, 467; *Muġnī,* VII, 4; *Tāğ,* II, 540, 541. The Sunnī al-Rāzī indiscriminately gives the definition of *kalāla* as the *awlād* and the *wālidān* (*Tafsīr Rāzī,* II, 378, 379) and as the *wālid* and the *walad* (*Tafsīr Rāzī,* II, 378, 575, 576).

[104] *Baḥr,* V, 346.

linguistic interest, since different doctrines proceed from different interpretations.

a) The grandfather

For Abū Bakr, Ibn ᶜAbbās, Ṭāwūs, al-Zuhrī, Qatāda, Dāwūd al-Ẓāhirī, the Ḥanafīs, Ẓāhirīs, and Ibāḍīs,[105] a grandfather has the same legal status as a father. Thus, he prevents the full or consanguine brothers and/or sisters from inheritance. Therefore, *kalāla* means the deceased person leaving neither sons, nor a father, nor a true grandfather; *walad* are only the male descendants, while *wālid* includes the father or a true grandfather. Regarding this, the Ḥanafī jurist al-Saraḫsī[106] says that *al-ǧadd* is like the *wālid* in the same manner as the son's son is like the son.

On the other hand, ᶜUmar, Sufyān al-Ṯawrī, al-Awzāᶜī, Ibrāhīm al-Naḫaᶜī, al-Šaybānī, Abū Yūsuf, Mālik and the Mālikīs, al-Šāfiᶜī and the Šāfiᶜīs, the Ḥanbalīs, and the Zaydīs, all hold that the grandfather inherits *together with* full or consanguine brothers and/or sisters. Thus *kalāla* means the deceased who has died leaving neither sons, nor sons' sons, nor a father;[107] *walad* is understood only as male children and *wālid* only as a father, even if these scholars also repeat the usual definition of *kalāla* as the deceased, either male or female, when he has died leaving neither *walad* nor *wālid.*[108] Consequently, daughters and the mother do not enter in the definition of *kalāla,* because, according to these scholars, full or consanguine brothers/sisters inherit with them.[109]

Mālik's reasoning is significant here. He states that the deceased is *kalāla* when, with respect to him, brothers are *ᶜaṣaba* if there is no *walad.*[110] As a matter of fact, full or consanguine brothers do not inherit if a son or a son of a son or a father is present.[111] If these heirs are dead, brothers are *ᶜaṣaba* with respect to the deceased.[112] In fact, full or consanguine brothers inherit together with the daughters and the son's daughters as agnates, that is, as *ᶜaṣaba bi-nafsihi.*[113]

If we consider the Iraqi opposition (Ibn Sīrīn al-Baṣrī, al-Ḥakam al-Kūfī, Šuᶜba al-Baṣrī, al-Šaybānī, and Abū Yūsuf), the Medinese opposi-

[105] *Dir. ered. II,* 268–69, 457; *Studies,* 1–32.
[106] *Šarḥ Siyar,* I, 227.
[107] *Dir. ered. II,* 269–72.
[108] *Šarḥ Zurqānī,* III, 105, 106.
[109] *Muġnī,* VII, 3–4.
[110] *Muwaṭṭaʾ,* III, 115.
[111] Ibid., 105.
[112] Ibid., 115.
[113] Ibid., 105.

tion (al-Zuhrī and Ibn Zayd), and the evolution inside the Meccan school,[114] we may conclude that the debate about the question of the grandfather began in the second half of the first century H. and that it was wholly concluded by the time of the Medinese Mālik and the Kūfan Abū Ḥanīfa.

b) ᶜAṣaba maᶜa ġayrihi

The principle of *ᶜaṣaba maᶜa ġayrihi* pertains in the case of two females inheriting together. *Per se,* a *ᶜāṣib* is a male, and thus only the *ᶜaṣaba bi-nafsihi* can rightly be called "agnates," a difficulty that is clearly reflected in the terminology. It is, of course, not necessary to specify that true agnates must be *bi-nafsihi* (*iure proprio*), as the term *ᶜaṣaba* is sufficient. The legal doctrine required, however, two other terms that were functions of the rule governing the particular case: *ᶜaṣaba bi-ġayrihi,* a daughter or a full or consanguine sister rendered agnates by their brothers, who are *ᶜaṣaba bi-nafsihi,* and *ᶜaṣaba maᶜa ġayrihi,* who are two females. The oddity of considering females agnates is apparent from the use of the masculine gender in both expressions. Moreover, it is only some later sources that make a distinction between agnates using this triple terminology (always in the masculine gender).[115]

As far as the *ᶜaṣaba maᶜa ġayrihi* is concerned, many ancient, as well as later, *ḥadīṯ* and juridical sources[116] simply do not deal with the question in any way, or merely discuss the doctrine without making use of special expressions. Some other sources[117] use a gender-specific expres-

---

[114] See chapter three.

[115] See *Mabsūṭ,* XXIX, 138; *Ḫulāṣa,* 207–8; *Šarḥ* of *Muqniᶜ,* II, 417; *Šarḥ Nīl,* VIII, 291, 292, 294.

[116] *Aḥkām, Āṯār, Fatāwā, Fiqh, Frühislamisches, Ǧāmiᶜ, Ǧāmiᶜ Ibn Baraka, Ǧāmiᶜ kabīr, Ḥuǧǧa, Iḥkām, Iḫtilāf Ṭaḥāwī, Masāʾil, Mudawwana, Mudawwana kubrā, Muḫtaṣar Qudūrī, Muṣannaf Kindī, Musnad Abī Ḥanīfa, Musnad Ḥumaydī, Musnad Šāfiᶜī, Muwaṭṭaʾ, Muwaṭṭaʾ Šaybānī, Risāla Šāfiᶜī¹, Risāla Šāfiᶜī², Šarḥ Muwaṭṭaʾ, Šarḥ Muwaṭṭaʾ Šaybānī, Šarḥ Siyar, Siyar, Sunna, Umm, ᶜUyūn.*

[117] *Aḥkām Qurʾān,* I, 654; *Baḥr,* V, 339, 340, 343; *Corpus,* 251; *Diritto,* 356; *Ḫizāna,* I, 414; *Ḫulāṣa,* 193, 205; *Kāfī,* II, 536; *Kifāya,* fol. 8v; *Mabsūṭ,* XXIX, 143, 156, 157, 158; *Minhāǧ,* II, 236–37; *Muġnī,* VII, 6; *Muḫtaṣar Basīwī,* 156; *Muḫtaṣar Ḫalīl,* II, 819; *Muḫtaṣar Ḫiraqī,* VII, 6; *Muḫtaṣar Ibrāhīm,* 206; *Muḫtaṣar Ṭaḥāwī,* 146; *Muqniᶜ,* II, 415; *Musnad Dārimī,* II, 251, no. 2884; *Nīl,* II, 381; *Risāla Qayrawānī,* 278/179; *Ṣaḥīḥ Buḫārī,* XXIII, 165 (in the title); *Šarḥ Nīl,* VIII, 293, 294, 295; *Sunan Bayhaqī,* VI, 233; *Tafsīr Ṭūsī,* III, 411; *Tuḥfa,* 892/893; *ᶜUmda,* 79; *Uṣūl,* fol. 128v.

sion such as *al-uḫt ᶜaṣaba maᶜa ᵓl-bint,* or something similar.[118] Some sources[119] use the unusual expressions *al-aḫawāt ᶜaṣabat al-banāt,* or *al-aḫawāt ᶜaṣaba liᵓl-banāt,*[120] which denote the strangeness of a female becoming an agnate through another female.

In contrast to the question of the grandfather, in the case of the *ᶜaṣaba maᶜa ġayrihi* there remained no divergences among the law schools, apart from the doctrine of some ancient scholars, as is seen in the *ḥadīṯ* literature that was followed in the Ẓāhirī school. According to Sunnīs, Zaydīs, and Ibāḍīs, a sister is considered as *ᶜaṣaba* if she inherits together with a daughter or a male descendant's daughter, however low. *Al-Muġnī*[121] has given a long list of authorities who agree with this doctrine: Zayd, Ibn ᶜAbbās, Ǧābir b. Zayd, al-Ḥasan, Qatāda, al-Naḫaᶜī, *ahl a-Madīna, ahl al-Baṣra,* and *ahl al-Kūfa.*

For the Ẓāhirīs, however, on the authority of Ibn ᶜAbbās and Ibn al-Zubayr,[122] as also in the *ḥadīṯ* literature, a sister is not considered *ᶜaṣaba* in this case; the remainder, after the allotment of the share to a daughter or to a son's daughter, goes to the *ᶜaṣaba.* But, adopting a compromise, they affirm that if there is no *ᶜāṣib,* the remainder is to be given to one or more full sisters or, in their absence, to one or more consanguine sisters.[123] The Ẓāhirī compromise is unknown in the Sunnī, Zaydī, and Ibāḍī law schools, and it has no basis in the *ḥadīṯ* literature. It is found in the *Muḥallā*[124] of Ibn Ḥazm (d. 456/1064), but it does not go back earlier than the latter years of the third century H., since it is unknown to a major Ẓāhirī work from that period, the *Masāᵓil* of *al-imām* Dāwūd al-Ẓāhirī (d. 270/884).[125] The Ẓāhirī reasoning is that a full or consanguine sister is an heir by quota if a person is inherited as *kalāla* because he died leaving neither a male nor a female *walad.* If, instead, a person, dying, leaves a female *walad,* the sister becomes an agnate, when there are no other male agnates having a right to the remainder after the allotment of the share to a daughter.

---

[118] or: *al-aḫawāt maᶜa ᵓl-banāt laysat bi-ᶜaṣaba* (*Masāᵓil Dāwūd,* 19; *Šarḥ Nīl,* VIII, 296).

[119] *Muḥallā,* IX, 256; *Muḫtaṣar Muzanī,* III, 143.

[120] *Aḥkām Qurᵓān,* I, 452.

[121] VII, 5–6.

[122] *Aḥkām Qurᵓān,* I, 452, 654; *Tafsīr Ṭabarī,* IX, 443–44.

[123] *Dir. ered. II,* 144.

[124] IX, 256–58, *masᵓala* 1712.

[125] *Masāᵓil Dāwūd,* 19.

Tafsīr Rāzī,[126] contradicting the Ismāᶜīlī and Imāmī definition of *kalāla* reported by him, agrees with the doctrine of the *ᶜaṣaba maᶜa ġayrihi.* He states that, if a deceased person leaves a daughter, a sister shall be entitled to receive one-half of the estate. The question is how the term *walad* must be understood. If it includes daughters as well as sons, they exclude sisters. If, instead, *walad* refers only to sons, sisters can inherit together with daughters.[127] According to *Tafsīr Nīsābūrī,*[128] *walad* must be interpreted only as *ibn* in this case.

The major interest of the *tafsīr* literature regards the reading of the verb *waraṯa*, the person or persons to whom the attribute *kalāla* applies, and why *kalāla* is in the accusative case in Qurʾān 4:12. The verb *waraṯa* can be read in at least two ways in this verse, and each reading is suited to a different attribution and etymology of the term *kalāla.* It is noteworthy that *ahl al-Baṣra* agree on the reading *yūraṯu,* which implies that *kalāla* is a quality of the deceased and that its etymology is from *kalla/yakillu,* as we already know from the *ḥadīṯ* literature; whereas the verb is read as *yūriṯu* by *ahl al-Kūfa, ahl al-Madīna,* and the Ḥiǧāzīs, so that the testimony of the *ḥadīṯ*s concerning the opinion of these scholars is confirmed, namely, that *kalāla* is a quality of the heirs and derives from *takallala.*

However the debate about the attribution and derivation of *kalāla* had no real consequence in the domain of the law. The jurists had the task of elaborating rules based on definitions. The law schools had therefore not only to formulate specific definitions of *kalāla* suited to their teachings on the grandfather and the *ᶜaṣaba maᶜa ġayrihi,* they also needed suitable definitions of the terms *walad* and *wālid,* which varied according to their doctrine. There was thus little consistency in their linguistic approach, which was dominated by juridical considerations.

---

[126] II, 575.
[127] *Tafsīr Manār,* VI, 109–10.
[128] VI, 35–36.

CHAPTER SIX

JURIDICAL ELABORATION ISMĀᶜĪLĪ AND IMĀMĪ SCHOOLS

SOURCES

Juridical works and ḥadīṯ *literature*

The sources examined here are the most important for the Ismāᶜīlī and the Imāmī schools of Šīᶜism. For the Ismāᶜīlīs, the basic works are those written by *al-qāḍī* Abū Ḥanīfa al-Nuᶜmān (d. 363/974): *Kitāb al-Iqtiṣār, Minhāǧ al-farāʾiḍ,* and *Muḫtaṣar al-āṯār.* As for the Imāmī sources, the most important are *al-Muqniᶜ waʾl-Hidāya* by Ibn Bābawayh (d. 381/991) and the *Kitāb al-Ḫilāf* by Šayḫ al-Ṭāʾifa al-Ṭūsī (d. 460/1067). In the *Šarāʾiᶜ al-Islām* by al-Ḥillī (d. 676/1277) there is nothing about *kalāla.*

The Ismāᶜīlī *Daᶜāʾim* by *al-qāḍī* Abū Ḥanīfa al-Nuᶜmān can be included in the *ḥadīṯ* literature, although it has only a limited number of recurring *isnād*s. The most ancient Imāmī traditionist work is *al-Uṣūl* of al-Kulaynī (d. 328/939). Also important are a number of works by Ibn Bābawayh, *ᶜIlal al-šarāʾiᶜ, Kitāb man lā yaḥḍuruhu ʾl-faqīh, Maᶜānī al-aḫbār,* and *Musnad al-imām Riḍā,* as well as the *Tahḏīb al-Aḥkām* and *al-Istibṣār* by al-Ṭūsī.

JURIDICAL DOCTRINE

The attribution of kalāla

The Ismāᶜīlī school ascribes the quality of *kalāla* to the deceased. Indeed, according to *Daᶜāʾim,*[1] "he (the deceased), dying, does not leave an inheritance as *kalāla* if he has left a mother or a father or a son or a daughter. Therefore, if he has left one of these, he is not the person designated by Allāh when he says, "Say: 'Allāh gives you a decision about the *kalāla*'" (Qurʾān 4:176). The ascription of the quality of *kalāla* to the deceased is more clear in another Ismāᶜīlī source, *Iqtiṣār,*[2] where it is said with reference to the inheritance of maternal half-siblings: "One-third of the estate shall be due to two or more maternal half-siblings if he (the deceased) has neither *walad* nor *wālid.*" Later on,[3] with reference to

---

[1] II, 372.

[2] p. 133.

[3] p. 134.

full siblings, it is stated: "If he (the deceased) does not leave either *walad* or *wālid,* full brothers and sisters have a right. . . ." The Imāmī school, however, is unanimous in asserting the doctrine that *kalāla* are brothers/ sisters and not the deceased.[4] The Šīᶜī jurist al-Ṭūsī[5] presented a thorough argument, which he arbitrarily attributed to Abū ᶜUbayda (d. 207/822), concerning the reason for considering brothers/sisters as *kalāla.* The argument, which is alien to the principles of the Sunnī schools, was reiterated by the Ḥanbalī jurist Ibn Qudāma,[6] who, thus, in this case, was clearly influenced by the Šīᶜī text,[7] as the Šīᶜī definition of *kalāla* quoted above in his *Muġnī* also shows.[8] According to this argument, bothers/sisters are *kalāla* if there are neither ascendants nor descendants with them. One says: "his kinship (*nasab*) has wound round him (*takallalahu*); the crown (*iklīl*) is so called because it encircles the head; it goes neither up nor down." This demonstrates that a brother is named *kalāla* if the deceased person lacks ascendants and descendants (his "extremities"). The doctrine is based on the verse of the poet al-Farazdaq discussed in chapter one.

Exclusion of brothers/sisters

Maternal half-siblings and full or paternal half-siblings:

kalāla = full or consanguine siblings when a person has died leaving neither *walad* nor *wālid*
walad = male and female descendants of any degree
wālid = father and mother

Ismāᶜīlī and Imāmī doctrine on *kalāla* is similar. The Imāmīs distinguish between *kalālat al-ab,* i.e., full or consanguine brothers/sisters,[9]

---

[4] *Ḫilāf,* II, 263–64; *Tafsīr Ṭūsī,* III, 135.

[5] *Ḫilāf,* II, 264.

[6] *Muġnī,* VII, 5.

[7] However, Ibn Qudāma makes no reference to Abū ᶜUbayda.

[8] On the lower margin of *Muqniᶜ* (II, 416–17) there is a text of Muḥammad b. ᶜAbd al-Wahhāb (d. 1206/1791) (*GAL,* II, 512; S, II, 530–31) in which he repeats the arguments of *Muġnī* on *kalāla.* He confirms the Šīᶜī definition of *kalāla;* but what is more surprising is that he gives a list of those scholars who supported it, which in no way corresponds to the data we know from the remaining sources; they are said to be Abū Bakr, Ibn ᶜAbbās, Zayd, Ǧābir b. Zayd, *ahl al-Madīna, ahl al-Baṣra,* and *ahl al-Kūfa.* No doubt Ibn ᶜAbd al-Wahhāb caused more confusion than Ibn Qudāma.

[9] *Ḫilāf,* II, 263, *masʾala* 26; *Istibṣār,* IV, 155; *Kitāb man,* IV, 201; *Muqniᶜ*

and *kalālat al-umm,* i.e., maternal half-siblings,[10] but both of them are subject to the same rules; that is, full, consanguine, and uterine brothers/sisters are precluded from inheritance by *wālidān,* i.e., father and mother, and by *walad,* i.e., the son (*ibn*) and the daughter (*ibna*), however low, or one of them. Thus, *kalāla* are brothers and sisters if a person has died leaving neither *walad* nor *wālidān.*[11] *Tafsīr Nīsābūrī*[12] says that "there is no doubt that brothers/sisters do not inherit in the presence of the parents (*abawān*), because the deceased is not *kalāla* if they are present." This doctrine is well synthesized in the statement of al-Ṭūsī:[13] brothers/sisters are named *kalāla* "because there are neither ascendants (*ᶜuluww*) nor descendants (*nuzūl*) with them (*lā yaᶜlū wa-lā yanzil*); but they are the surroundings (*wasaṭ*)." "If a man has died leaving a mother or a father or a son or a daughter, we are not dealing with those designated by Allāh in Qurʾān 4:176" (*isnād* 34). The same rule might be presented in various ways. So we can say that only a wife and husband inherit together with a mother and a father (*wālidān, abawān*), or a son and a daughter (*walad*)[14] (*isnād* 34[15]), because, if they are present, we are not dealing

---

Ibn Bābawayh, 175; *Uṣūl Kulaynī,* VII, 74, 83. Al-Ḥillī makes a better distinction between *kalālat al-ab waʾl-umm* (*Šarāʾiᶜ,* IV, 26, 27, 29) and *kalālat al-ab* (*Šarāʾiᶜ,* IV, 26, 27, 29, 30).

[10] *Ḫilāf,* II, 263, *masʾala* 26; *Istibṣār,* IV, 159; *Kitāb man,* IV, 201; *Muqniᶜ Ibn Bābawayh,* 175; *Šarāʾiᶜ,* IV, 10, 21, 27, 29, 62; *Uṣūl Kulaynī,* VII, 83.

[11] *Āṯār Nuᶜmān,* fols. 118v, 119r, 121v; *Daᶜāʾim,* II, 371–72, no. 1339; 375, no. 1345; *Iqtiṣār,* 133, 134; *Maǧmaᶜ,* II, 149; *Minhāǧ Nuᶜmān,* fol. 2v; *Ḫilāf,* II, 263, *masʾala* 25; 264, *masʾala* 27; *Istibṣār,* IV, 146, no. 548; *Kitāb man,* IV, 196, no. 673; 202; 203; *Ṣaḥīḥ,* III, 274, no. 3953; *Tafsīr Ṭūsī,* III, 138, 408, 409; *Tahḏīb Ṭūsī,* IX, 250; 292; *Uṣūl Kulaynī,* VII, 71, 74, 82, 83, 87, 92, 99, no. 1. A number of cases regarding the exclusion of brothers and sisters by descendants and ascendants are solved; cf. *Āṯār Nuᶜmān,* fol. 118v; *Daᶜāʾim,* II, 371–72, no. 1339; *Minhāǧ Nuᶜmān,* fols. 11v–12v; *Ḫilāf,* II, 266, *masʾala* 36; 266–67, *masʾala*s 37–38; 267, *masʾala*s 42–44; 270, *masʾala*s 55–56; 273, *masʾala* 68; 290, *masʾala* 104; 291–92, *masʾala*s 106–7; 295, *masʾala* 112; 306, *masʾala* 150; *Istibṣār,* IV, 145–46, nos. 546–47; 147, no. 552; 161, no. 608; 167, no. 632; *Kitāb man,* IV, 190; 191, no. 661, 663–64; 196, no. 673; 197–98; *Muqniᶜ Ibn Bābawayh,* 171–72, 172; *Musnad Riḍā,* II, 435, no. 12; *Ṣaḥīḥ,* III, 267, no. 3936; *Šarāʾiᶜ,* IV, 21, 22, 24; *Tahḏīb Ṭūsī,* IX, 254; 270, no. 981; 273, no. 986; 278, nos. 1005–6; 278–79, no. 1009, 1012; 280–81, no. 1014; 283–84, nos. 1023–26; 286, no. 1037; 290, no. 1044; 317, no. 1140; 321–22, no. 1153; *Uṣūl Kulaynī,* VII, 87, no. 4; 91, no. 2; 91–92, no. 1.

[12] IV, 201.

[13] *Ḫilāf,* II, 263–64.

[14] *Āṯār Nuᶜmān,* fol. 118v; *Daᶜāʾim,* II, 371–72, no. 1339; *Iqtiṣār,* 133;

with *kalāla;*[16] or, that only parents (*abawān*), and a wife and a husband, can inherit together with a *walad* (*isnād* 35[17]).

The *rağul*s cited in the chain of transmitters of these two *ḥadīṯ*s are generally considered *ṯiqa;* for instance, Muḥammad b. Muslim al-Kūfī[18] (d. 150/767), Ğamīl,[19] Aḥmad b. Muḥammad b. Abī Naṣr al-Kūfī[20] (d. 221/836), Ibrāhīm b. al-Ḥusayn b. ᶜAlī al-Madanī,[21] Aḥmad b. Muḥammad b. ᶜĪsā al-Qummī,[22] ᶜAlī b. Ibrāhīm[23] (all in *isnād* 34), ᶜAlī b. Saᶜīd,[24] Mūsā b. Bakr,[25] Ṣafwān al-Kūfī[26] (d. 210/825–26), al-Ḥasan b. Muḥammad b. Samāᶜa al-Kūfī[27] (d. 263/876–77), and Ḥumayd b. Ziyād al-Kūfī[28] (d. 310/922–23) (all in *isnād* 35). On the contrary, Muslim critics expressed a very negative judgment regarding Sahl b. Ziyād (*isnād* 34).[29]

Minhāğ Nuᶜmān, fol. 4v; *Hidāya,* 82; *Kitāb man,* IV, 189, 190, 196; *Ṣaḥīḥ,* III, 263, nos. 3920–21; *Šarāʾiᶜ,* IV, 17; *Tahḏīb Ṭūsī,* IX, 251, nos. 969–70; *Uṣūl Kulaynī,* VII, 82–83, no. 1, 83. Because of their peculiar doctrine, Ismāᶜīlīs also maintain that the grandmother can inherit together with the *wālidān* and *walad;* cf. *Āṯār Nuᶜmān,* fol. 118v; *Iqtiṣār,* 133; *Minhāğ Nuᶜmān,* fol. 4v; cf. also *Dir. ered. I,* 117–18.

[15] *Uṣūl Kulaynī* (VII, 82–83, no. 1) and *Ṣaḥīḥ* (III, 263, no. 3920), in the *isnād,* have "Abū Ayyūb and others," and the *matn* relates only the first sentence; while *Uṣūl Kulaynī* (VII, 99, no. 1), *Ṣaḥīḥ* (III, 274, no. 3953), and *Tahḏīb Ṭūsī* (IX, 319, no. 1145; with the *isnād* lacking "Ibrāhīm"), in the *isnād,* have "Abū Ayyūb and ᶜAbd Allāh b. Bakīr," and the *matn* relates only the second sentence. Finally, *Uṣūl Kulaynī* (VII, 83), and *Ṣaḥīḥ* (III, 263, no. 3921) have both sentences.

[16] *Ṣaḥīḥ,* III, 263, no. 3921; *Tahḏīb Ṭūsī,* IX, 251, no. 970; *Uṣūl Kulaynī,* VII, 83.

[17] With a different *isnād,* also in *ᶜIlal,* 569; *Kitāb man,* IV, 189; *Tahḏīb Ṭūsī,* IX, 249–50, no. 964.

[18] One of the most prominent Šīᶜī scholars in Kūfa, a companion of Abū Ğaᶜfar and Abū ᶜAbd Allāh (*Riğāl Ḥillī,* 149–50; *Riğāl Nağāšī,* 226–27).

[19] He died in the time of al-Riḍā (*Riğāl Nağāšī,* 92).

[20] Ibid., 54.

[21] *Riğāl,* 144.

[22] *Riğāl Ḥillī,* 13–14.

[23] Ibid., 100.

[24] *Riğāl Nağāšī,* 183.

[25] Ibid., 290.

[26] Ibid., 139–40.

[27] *Riğāl Ḥillī,* 212; *Riğāl Nağāšī,* 29–31.

[28] *Riğāl Ḥillī,* 59; *Riğāl Nağāšī,* 95–96.

[29] He was considered very weak and not reliable (*ġayr muᶜtamad*) in *ḥadīṯ;*

ᶜAṣaba maᶜa ġayrihi*: the doctrine excluded*

The consequence of the Ismāᶜīlī and Imāmī interpretation of the term *kalāla* is that the doctrine of *ᶜaṣaba maᶜa ġayrihi* is excluded.[30] According to the Ismāᶜīlī and Imāmī schools, "the Prophetic *ḥadīṯ, al-aḫawāt maᶜa ʾl-banāt ᶜaṣaba,* is a *ḫabar wāḥid* that must not be taken into account because it contradicts an explicit Qurʾānic text" (*Sūra* 4:176).[31] Thus, in the case of a daughter, a son's daughter, and a full or consanguine sister, the sister does not inherit because the daughters prevent sisters; they are not *ᶜaṣaba* in the presence of the daughters. This solution is attributed to Ibn Masᶜūd and Ibn ᶜAbbās.[32] However, whereas for Ibn ᶜAbbās we have numerous and various supporting examples, for Ibn Masᶜūd, on the contrary, we find some reports supporting *ᶜaṣaba maᶜa ġayrihi* and others rejecting it.[33] Al-Ṭūsī[34] himself, in some places, does not attribute this specific doctrine to Ibn Masᶜūd, but only to Ibn ᶜAbbās. The doctrine of the *ᶜaṣaba maᶜa ġayrihi* was also denied by ᶜAbd Allāh b. al-Zubayr, Ǧābir b. ᶜAbd Allāh, and Dāwūd,[35] as we have already discovered in the Sunnī sources.

If we consider the definition of *kalāla* in the two *ḥadīṯ*s having *isnād*s 36 and 37, we note that it corresponds to the Iraqi one, and the same definition is repeated in some juridical as well as *tafsīr* works.[36] Thus, it is only a question of the interpretation of the words *walad* and *wālid.* That this is the problem is demonstrated by the fact that *al-qāḍī* al-Nuᶜmān,[37] speaking about brothers/sisters of any kind being precluded

---

his reports and his *maḏhab* were *fāsid;* he related *ḥadīṯ mursal* and relied on unknown persons (*maǧāhīl*); he was charged with *kaḏib* (falsehood) (*Riǧāl Ḥillī,* 228–29; *Riǧāl Naǧāšī,* 132).

[30] *Daᶜāʾim,* II, 366–69, nos. 1331–32; *Ḫilāf,* II, 273, *masʾala* 67; 279; *Maǧmaᶜ,* II, 149; *Ṣaḥīḥ,* III, 265, nos. 3926, 3929; 275, no. 3956; *Tafsīr Ṭūsī,* III, 408, 411; *Tahḏīb Ṭūsī,* IX, 250, 264; *Uṣūl Kulaynī,* VII, 87, nos. 5, 8; 99–100, nos. 1, 2; 104, no. 8.

[31] *Maǧmaᶜ,* II, 149; *Tafsīr Ṭūsī,* III, 411.

[32] *Ḫilāf,* II, 273, *masʾala* 67.

[33] *Tafsīr Nīsābūrī,* VI, 35–36.

[34] *Ḫilāf,* II, 273, *masʾala* 67; 307, *masʾala* 152; *Maǧmaᶜ,* II, 149; *Tafsīr Ṭūsī,* III, 411.

[35] *Ḫilāf,* II, 276, *masʾala* 80. *Ḫilāf* (II, 307, *masʾala* 152) quotes only Ibn ᶜAbbās.

[36] *ᶜIlal,* 569; *Kitāb man,* IV, 189; *Tahḏīb Ṭūsī,* IX, 250; *Uṣūl Kulaynī,* VII, 74.

[37] *Daᶜāʾim,* II, 375, no. 1345.

from inheritence "by *wālid, walad,* a mother and a daughter," refers to an inclusive definition of *kalāla.* Significantly al-Nuᶜmān needs to add "mother and daughter" in order to specify the purport of the definition, maybe in contrast with Sunnīs, Zaydīs, Ẓāhirīs, and Ibāḍīs, because "mother" is not included in the term *"wālid,"* and because "daughter" is not considered as *"walad"* by them. Al-Ṭūsī[38] (d. 460/1067) attributes the definition of *kalāla* as "the parents (*wālidān*)" to al-Qutaybī[39] (d. 276/889), and the definition of *kalāla* as "the parents (*wālidān*) and offspring (*mawlūdūn*)" to Abū ᶜUbayda al-Baṣrī (d. 207/822). However this is only an attempt to bestow legitimacy on a doctrine of his school. In fact, as far as al-Qutaybī is concerned, such a definition is attributed to him in no other linguistic, *ḥadīṯ,* or juridical work examined here; and as for Abū ᶜUbayda, in a more ancient work than *Ḫilāf,*[40] he considers *kalāla* as "a person who has neither *walad,* nor a father, *nor a brother* as heirs (emphasis mine)."

A debate with the Sunnīs on the doctrine of *ᶜaṣaba maᶜa ġayrihi* is presented by al-Faḍl b. Šāḏān al-Nīsābūrī (d. 260/874),[41] a disciple of ᶜAlī al-Riḍā.[42] He repeats the position of his school, proving it on the basis of the interpretation of the word *walad,* which includes male as well as female descendants, however low; likewise *al-wālidān,* or one of them, inhibit any kind of brothers/sisters from inheritance. According to al-Faḍl, the Sunnī doctrine "is in opposition to (*ḫālafa*) Allāh and his Messenger" and is based neither on "the Qurᵓān, nor on a *sunna ğāmiᶜa,* nor on a *qiyās.*"[43]

---

[38] *Ḫilāf,* II, 263.

[39] He is the well known author Ibn Qutayba; see *GAS,* VIII, 337, s.v. "al-Qutaibī."

[40] Cf. *Tahḏīb luġa,* IX, 447; it is repeated in *Lisān,* XI, 592.

[41] *Uṣūl Kulaynī,* VII, 105.

[42] *GAL,* I, 199, no. 2a; S, III, 1201, no. 2a; *GAS,* I, 537–38, no. 27; *Riğāl Ḥillī,* 132–33; *Riğāl Nağāšī,* 216–17.

[43] Although the Imāmī definition of *kalāla* is similar to the Iraqi one, the transmitters are not the same. Nevertheless, they are considered as *ṯiqa;* for instance, Ḥamza b. Ḥumrān b. Aᶜyan al-Kūfī (*Riğāl,* 118, 177), ᶜAlī b. Ribāṭ al-Kūfī (*Riğāl,* 384; *Riğāl Ḥillī,* 99–100), ᶜAbd al-Raḥmān b. al-Ḥağğāğ al-Kūfī (*Riğāl Ḥillī,* 113–14; *Riğāl Nağāšī,* 165), Muḥammad b. Abī ᶜUmayr al-Baġdādī (d. 217/832; *Riğāl Nağāšī,* 228–30), Yaᶜqūb b. Yazīd (*Riğāl Nağāšī,* 313), al-Faḍl b. Šāḏān (d. 260/874), and Zurāra b. Aᶜyan al-Kūfī (d. 150/767; *Fihrist Ṭūsī,* 74–75, no. 302; *Riğāl,* 123, no. 16; 201, no. 90; 350, no. 1; *Riğāl Nağāšī,* 125).

CASES SOLVED IN OPPOSITION TO IMĀMĪ DOCTRINE

While the Ismāᶜīlīs generally base their univocal doctrine on the authority of Ǧaᶜfar b. Muḥammad,[44] or on the *isnād:* Ǧaᶜfar b. Muḥammad ← his father ← his ancestors ← ᶜAlī ← the Messenger of God,[45] there is a more complex situation in the Imāmī school. In fact, in the Imāmī works some reports contradict the established doctrine of the school. Two preliminary points should be made here. Firstly, any reference to the main Imāmī authorities (i.e., Abū ᶜAbd Allāh and Abū Ǧaᶜfar) is fictitious, even though the *isnād*s of the Imāmī traditions almost always begin with one of their names, and even though there are no divergences in the school on the doctrines reported from them, as Zurāra says (*isnād* 35). Secondly, although according to al-Ṭūsī, the divergences within the school are due to *taqiyya,* I believe they represent valuable elements in outlining the history of its doctrine.

Some cases are clearly solved contrary to Imāmī doctrine or reveal a debate inside the Imāmī school. Eight such cases will be recounted in the following pages.

1) In a case (mother, brothers, and sisters inheriting together), submitted to al-Riḍā by Muḥammad b. Ismāᶜīl b. Bazīᶜ, one-sixth is given to the mother and the remainder to the brothers and sisters (*isnād* 38), as is the rule according to the Sunnī, Zaydī, Ẓāhirī, and Ibāḍī schools.[46] Al-Riḍā[47] died in the year 203/818. This means that in the Imāmī school, the doctrine of the exclusion of brothers/sisters by the mother was not accepted at the beginning of the third century H.

2) Zurāra b. Aᶜyan asked Abū ᶜAbd Allāh about a woman who had died leaving her husband, her mother, her uterine brothers, and her full brothers. He answered: "One-half shall be due to the husband, one-sixth to the mother, and one-third to the uterine brothers, while full brothers are excluded" (*isnād* 39).[48]

This is the well-known case called *mušarraka,* and it is solved in accordance with Ḥanafī, Ḥanbalī, and Zaydī doctrine.[49] What is important here is that the mother does not exclude all brothers, contrary to the doctrine of the Imāmī school. Al-Ṭūsī's explanation is that this report "is not

---

[44] *Daᶜāʾim,* II, 366–67, no. 1331; 371–72, no. 1339; 375, no. 1345.

[45] *Daᶜāʾim,* II, 371–72, no. 1339.

[46] For the *isnād,* Muḥammad b. Ismāᶜīl b. Bazīᶜ was considered as *ṯiqa, ṣaḥīḥ,* and he was a prominent person (*ᶜayn*) (*Riǧāl Ḥillī,* 139–40).

[47] *GAL,* I, 199, no. 2; S, I, 318–19, no. 2; *GAS,* I, 535–36, no. 22.

[48] *Istibṣār,* no. 549; *Tahḏīb Ṭūsī,* no. 1049, no. 1152.

[49] Cf. *Dir. ered. II,* 219–23.

in force in the school because the well-established Imāmī doctrine is that the presence of the mother causes the exclusion of all brothers."[50] According to him, the report was probably due to *taqiyya.*

3) The following case has the same *isnād* as the preceding one: "A woman dies leaving her mother, her full sisters, her uterine brothers, and her consanguine sisters: two-thirds shall be due to the full sisters, one-sixth to the mother, and one-sixth to the uterine brothers"; consanguine sisters are excluded (*isnād* 39).[51]

We face a solution that is neither Sunnī nor Šīcī. As a matter of fact, the Sunnī, Zaydī, and Ibāḍī solution is to give one-third, instead of one-sixth, to the uterine brothers; then they have recourse to *cawl.*[52] As for the Ismācīlīs and Imāmīs, the mother prevents any kind of brother/sister from inheritance; in the absence of the mother and with the application of *cawl,* only the share of the full sisters is reduced, while the uterine brothers have a right to their full quota of one-third.[53] So the damage falls only on full or consanguine brothers/sisters when the estate is insufficient to cover all the shares, as Ibn cAbbās, Dāwūd, and the Ẓāhirī school hold.[54] In the case considered here, in contrast with Imāmī doctrine, the mother does not exclude brothers/sisters.

In the *isnād,* the following *rağul*s are mentioned: Muṯannā al-Ḥannāṭ al-Kūfī,[55] al-Ḥasan b. cAlī al-Ḫazzāz b. Faḍḍāl al-Kūfī[56] (d. 224/838–39), and cAlī b. al-Ḥakam.[57]

However, al-Ṭūsī[58] remarks that Zurāra is at the origin (*aṣl*) of both of the preceding traditions and that the channel of transmission (*ṭarīq*) is unique, that furthermore the Imāmī school is in agreement on proceeding in opposition to such a doctrine, and that the divergence was probably due either to *taqiyya* or to a license (*ruḫṣa*) to adopt from the Sunnīs what they believe.

I believe that it was not a matter of *ruḫṣa,* because the solution is not

---

[50] *Tahḏīb Ṭūsī,* IX, 293, 321. For the Imāmī doctrine, see *Dir. ered. I,* 81, and n. 22.

[51] *Istibṣār,* nos. 550–51; *Tahḏīb Ṭūsī,* nos. 1149–51.

[52] *Dir. ered. II,* 244

[53] *Dir. ered. I,* 25–28.

[54] *Dir. ered. II,* 63.

[55] A disciple of Ğacfar al-Ṣādiq, who very probably died in the second half of the second century H. (*GAS,* I, 533, no. 14; *Riğāl Nağāšī,* 294–95).

[56] *Riğāl Nağāšī,* 24–26.

[57] Ibid., 195.

[58] *Istibṣār,* IV, 147.

completely Sunnī. The only certainty is that in the Imāmī school there was for a long time no fixed doctrine and that references to Abū ᶜAbd Allāh and Abū Ǧaᶜfar, such as the reference to Abū ᶜAbd Allāh at the beginning of the *isnād,* are fictitious.

4) On the authority of Abū ᶜAbd Allāh, the case of "a man who has died leaving his mother, his wife, his [full or consanguine] sister, and his grandfather" is solved giving "one-third to the mother, one-fourth to the wife, while the remainder is to be divided among the sister and the grandfather, giving to the male the double share of a female" (*isnād* 40).[59] This solution is according to Mālikī, Šāfiᶜī, and Ḥanbalī doctrine.[60]

5) A variation of the previous case is solved on the authority of Abū Ǧaᶜfar: "If a man dies leaving his mother, his wife, two [full or consanguine] sisters, and his grandfather, one-sixth shall be due to the mother, one-fourth to the wife, while the remainder shall be divided among the sisters and the grandfather, giving to the grandfather the double share of a sister" (*isnād* 40).[61] This solution is also that of the Mālikī, Šāfiᶜī, and Ḥanbalī schools.[62]

Al-Ṭūsī comments that "these two traditions (*ḫabar*) were ignored (*matrūk*) on the basis of the *iǧmāᶜ* of the school. Indeed, according to Imāmī doctrine, neither brothers or sisters of any kind, nor grandfather or grandmother, inherit together with both parents (*abawān*) or one of them." For al-Ṭūsī, the origin of those two traditions lies in "*taqiyya,* because they agree with the *maḏhab* of the *ᶜāmma.*"[63] However, what is important for us is that for a certain time, impossible to establish exactly, some scholars inside the Imāmī school followed the Sunnī doctrine.

6) A series of *ḥadīṯ*s reveals a debate concerning one of the main areas of divergence between the Ismāᶜīlī and Imāmī schools and the remaining law schools. It can be summarized in three questions: 1) Do uterine brothers cause *ḥaǧb nuqṣān* (partial reduction) of the mother's share from a one-third to one-sixth, even if they do not inherit because of the presence of the father? 2) Can uterine brothers inherit together with the mother if the father is not present? 3) What kind of brothers/sisters can partially exclude the mother?

Zurāra solves the case of a person who has died leaving parents and uterine brothers in accordance with Sunnī, Zaydī, Ẓāhirī, and Ibāḍī doc-

---

59 no. 611.

60 *Dir. ered. II,* 317.

61 no. 612.

62 *Dir. ered. II,* 318.

63 *Istibṣār,* IV, 161–62.

trine: one-sixth shall be due to the mother and the remainder to the father; thus, the mother is partially excluded from 1/3 to 1/6 by uterine brothers. But in the same *matn,* Abū cAbd Allāh, the chief Imāmī authority, reaffirms the Imāmī doctrine[64] (*isnād* 41).[65]

This *matn* seems to be simply a rejection of Zurāra. This conclusion is confirmed by another report where cUbayd b. Zurāra, his son, directly relates, on the authority of Abū cAbd Allāh, that uterine brothers do not partially exclude the mother from her share of one-third (*isnād* 42). It is quite impossible to give information about the origin of this *ḥadīṯ;* the only thing one can say with any certainty is that there was doctrinal opposition inside the Imāmī school. The report has a family *isnād:* cUbayd,[66] a son of Zurāra, transmitted the *matn* to his paternal uncle, cAbd Allāh b. Bakīr,[67] a brother of Zurāra. It seems that some family names were used in order to detract from the position of Zurāra. Furthermore, the doctrine is attributed to a major authority, Abū cAbd Allāh, rather than to Zurāra. This fact that the argument proceeds along this line lends no credibility to the report.

Lastly, Zurāra asked cAlī b. Sacīd about this case, who solved it in accordance with Sunnī doctrine, but Zurāra himself disapproves of the solution and broadly explains Imāmī doctrine (*isnād* 43). Notice that the first three *rağul*s of *isnād* 43 are the same as in *isnād* 35, where Imāmī doctrine is discussed in detail. Another tradition attributes the standard doctrine of the Imāmī school to Zurāra: in the presence of the father, uterine brothers neither exclude the mother nor inherit, while full or consanguine brothers partially exclude the mother from one-third to one-sixth, but they do not inherit. In the absence of the father, on the other hand, no kind of brother/sister either excludes the mother or inherits, because they are not *kalāla*[68] (*isnād* 44). In the *isnād,* cUmar b. Uḏayna al-Baṣrī[69] and Muḥammad b. Abī cUmayr[70] (d. 217/832) appear.

---

[64] For the Imāmī doctrine, see *Ḫilāf,* II, 265, *mas*ᵓ*ala* 32; *Istibṣār,* IV, 142; *Kitāb man,* 197, 198; *Muqni*c *Ibn Bābawayh,* 170; *Šarā*ᵓ*i*c, IV, 19, 20. Also the Ḥanafī jurist al-Saraḫsī (*Mabsūṭ,* XXIX, 145) relates the Imāmī doctrine, with the same rationale; however, he attributes it to the *Zaydiyya.*

[65] In the *isnād,* al-Ḥusayn b. Sacīd (he was alive around the year 300/913) was Kūfan (*GAS,* I, 539, no. 31; *Riğāl Nağāšī,* 42–45). Likewise, Ḥarīz belonged to *ahl al-Kūfa* (*Riğāl Nağāšī,* 105).

[66] *Riğāl Nağāšī,* 162.

[67] *Riğāl,* 225; *Riğāl Ḥillī,* 106–7; *Riğāl Nağāšī,* 154.

[68] *Istibṣār* (IV, 145, no. 545) has only the second part of this *matn.*

[69] He wrote a *Kitāb al-Farā*ᵓ*iḍ* (*Riğāl Nağāšī,* 202).

In brief, *isnād*s 41–44 constitute a doctrinal development allegedly instituted by Zurāra, but that was perhaps the reflection of a current inside the Imāmī school. The four *ḥadīṯ*s examined above would seem to underline a doctrinal evolution from the negation to the acceptance of the Imāmī doctrine, probably during the third century H.

Regarding the other specifically Imāmī doctrine, namely, that the mother excludes any kind of brother/sister from inheritance,[71] evidence suggests that for a long time it was the object of uncertainty. In fact, Ibn Bābawayh[72] (d. 381/991) reports that, according to al-Faḍl b. Šāḏān (d. 260/874), the mother excludes *uterine brothers* from inheritance without mentioning full or consanguine brothers. Does this mean that the doctrine was not fixed in some Šīᶜī circles at the time of al-Faḍl b. Šāḏān? Moreover, Ibn Bābawayh[73] relates a doctrine according to which the mother is excluded from her one-third share by brothers, but without specifying the kind of brothers. Does this mean that the Imāmī doctrine was not yet fully accepted even more than a century later in his time?

7) A long tradition (*isnād* 45), with almost the same chain of transmitters as *isnād* 44, reveals a broad debate concerning the divergences regarding *kalāla* that seems to me too developed to have originated at such an early date. It reportedly takes place between Zurāra, who reaffirms the Imāmī doctrine, and some anonymous Sunnīs. Zurāra introduces his argument with: *qulnā* ("we said" or "we replied"); however the words may not be those of Zurāra, but of anonymous Imāmī scholars. Let us follow Zurāra's reasoning, based on his *raʾy.* According to the Sunnīs, in the case of one or more daughters and a full or consanguine brother or a full or consanguine sister, one or more daughters have the right, respectively, to one-half or to two-thirds, while the remainder is to be given to the brother as *ᶜaṣaba iure proprio* or to the sister as *ᶜaṣaba maᶜa ġayrihi,* the remaining *ᶜaṣaba iure proprio,* such as paternal cousins or brother's sons, being excluded, whereas uterine brothers/sisters are barred from inheritance by the presence of one or more daughters. Zurāra wonders why one excludes uterine brothers, but not full or consanguine brothers/sisters. The Sunnī solution distinguishes between Qurʾān 4:12 and 4:17, although the same term, *kalāla,* is used in both verses. Zurāra rejects the distinction. Imāmīs and Sunnīs agree on the fact that father and sons exclude all collaterals; but they diverge regarding mother and

---

[70] *Riǧāl Ḥillī,* 140–41.

[71] See *ᶜIlal,* 569; *Tahḏīb Ṭūsī,* IX, 249–50, no. 964.

[72] *Kitāb man,* IV, 189.

[73] Ibid.

daughters. While both Imāmīs and Sunnīs maintain that uterine brothers are excluded by daughters, Imāmīs reject the Sunnī doctrine that attributes one-third to the uterine brothers/sisters in the presence of the mother. How can the Sunnī teaching be correct, Zurāra says, if uterine brothers/sisters inherit by means of their mother's right? Full and consanguine brothers/sisters, meanwhile, are barred by the father, as they inherit through his right. Lastly, Zurāra rejects the Sunnī doctrine that uterine brothers are excluded by the presence of daughters, whereas, at the same time, they partially exclude the mother from one-third to one-sixth.

Such a debate presumably cannot go back to Zurāra (d. 150/767), because we have no evidence of it in other than Šīᶜī sources. Most probably the discussion precedes the final acceptance of the standard doctrine of his school. However this may be, it is important to bear in mind that the discussion always turns on the interpretation of the terms *walad* and *wālid.*

8) The application of the Imāmī doctrine was not so rigid that it completely rejected Sunnī rule in interconfessional relations. As a matter of fact, Ibn Muḥriz asked Abū ᶜAbd Allāh about a daughter and a sister. He allotted the whole estate to the daughter, according to the Imāmī doctrine. But Ibn Muḥriz objected that the deceased belonged to those people (Sunnīs?), while the sister was *muʾmina ᶜārifa.* Then Abū ᶜAbd Allāh allotted only one-half to her. Ibn Uḏayna mentioned this to Zurāra, who agreed with Ibn Muḥriz (*isnād* 46). It seems to me that this report reflects a situation in which there was not yet a sharp division between Sunnīs and Šīᶜīs.

What distinguishes Sunnī and Šīᶜī doctrine is not so much the definition of the term *kalāla,* as the explanation of the terms *walad* and *wālid* contained in that definition. However, even if, in contradistinction to the Sunnīs, *walad* is correctly interpreted by the Imāmīs and the Ismāᶜīlīs as male and female descendants—with the consequent exclusion of the doctrine of the *ᶜaṣaba maᶜa ġayrihi*—the term *wālid* is improperly extended by them also to the mother. The attempt to bestow legitimacy on the definition of *kalāla* as "the parents" (al-Qutaybī), or as "the parents and offspring" (Abū ᶜUbayda), has no foundation in the most ancient sources. That the Šīᶜī doctrine before the third century H. was the same as that of the Sunnīs, or that it was as yet uncertain, is proved by a series of cases found in the Šīᶜī sources themselves. The change in the Imāmī doctrine may be fictitiously attributed to Zurāra (d. 150/767), who was a pre-eminent scholar of the second century H. and who solved some cases according to Sunnī doctrine. It seems more precise to maintain that a debate about the two terms of *walad* as male and female ascendants, and of *wālid* as father and mother, occurred at the time of Ibn Šāḏān (d. 260/874). Thus it is probable that the Imāmī and Ismāᶜīlī systems of law began to be formed during the first half of the third century H.

CONCLUSIONS

The individual interpretations of the term *kalāla* given by the law schools were not merely part of an academic discussion, rather they allowed the jurists to create new rules that partly modify the Qurʾānic provisions in order to solve new cases. In other words, the few Qurʾānic verses on inheritance did not suffice to form a complete system. Some legal problems arose after the Prophet's era and they were solved by means of interpretation. In particular, the different explanations of the term *kalāla* given by the law schools reflect the different solutions given to the questions about the position of the grandfather in the law of inheritance and to the case of full or consanguine sisters inheriting with daughters. While the literal sense of the Qurʾānic verses requires that the grandfather be treated as the father according to the pre-Islamic agnate rule, with the consequent exclusion of all siblings, in the two centers of Iraq and Medina there was a doctrinal elaboration that adapted these Qurʾānic rules to a fair solution based on justice. There is no evidence that such doctrines are legal borrowings; they are absolutely consistent with the principles of Islamic law and move completely inside an Arab and Islamic way of thinking. The *ḥadīṯ* literature represents an intermediate stage between the data of the revelation and the juridical elaboration; it forms the background for the subsequent legal debate.

In this context, I do not give much importance to the exact dating of the *ḥadīṯ*s. For convenience, I have followed Schacht's method, which seems to give good results as regards the *ḥadīṯ*s on *kalāla,* but it cannot be generally applicable; maybe there is no definite method for dating *ḥadīṯ*s. What I believe important is to point out that the *ḥadīṯ*s investigated in this study originated in general about the end of the first century and the beginning of the second century H.; thus we might suppose that during the first decades of Islam the Qurʾānic rules were literally followed; later on, based on principles of equity, some objections began to emerge about the exclusion of brothers/sisters, who are Qurʾānic heirs, because of the presence of the grandfather, who is not mentioned in the Qurʾān, and about the exclusion of full or consanguine sisters, who are Qurʾānic heirs, because of the presence of the daughters, in favor of more distant relatives, namely, the *ʿaṣaba* or the *ḏawū ʾl-arḥām.*

Based on the various kind of sources so far examined, a series of conclusions can be drawn. The main intent of the traditionists, as it is evidenced in the *ḥadīṯ* literature, was to support, based on their own *raʾy,* a particular doctrinal view. At first sight, it seems strange that the Medinese school did not have a clear definition of *kalāla.* Nevertheless, each school needed to give its own definition, stressing the meaning of the terms *walad* and *wālid.* In fact, the juridical elaboration too, likewise on the basis of *raʾy,* rendered the contents of the term *kalāla* explicit, specifying above all the implication of the words *walad* and *wālid.*

Why did Sunnīs, Zaydīs, and Ibāḍīs distinguish between the two Qurʾānic verses, applying different doctrines, if the same term is used? Surely the position of the Ismāʿīlīs and Imāmīs, who gave the same meaning to the term in both verses is more consistent. Are the Ismāʿīlī and Imāmī definitions of *walad* as both male and female children, and of *wālid* as father and mother, linguistically correct? The Ẓāhirīs also gave the same meaning to *kalāla* in both verses, and they almost give *kalāla* the meaning that reflects its original linguistic definition. But they likewise admit, in a particular case, the doctrine of the *ʿaṣaba maʿa ġayrihi.*

It seems sure that *kalāla* does not express a direct link between a person and his kinship (ascendants and descendants); on the contrary, it is *mā yattaṣilu biʾl-wāsiṭa* (two relatives linked to each other through another relative); thus it refers to *qarāba baʿīda* when there is no *walad* or *wālid,* because of the weakness caused by the absence of the kinship of the ascendants (*uṣūl*) and the descendants (*furūʿ*).[1] The ascription of the quality of *kalāla* is different according to the grammar school of Baṣra (*kalāla* is the deceased) and the grammar school of Kūfa (collaterals are *kalāla*); but, as seems attested by all the poetic verses here examined, from the linguistic point of view one should opt for *kalāla* as referring to collaterals. However, from the doctrinal point of view, what we need is to establish the meaning of *walad* and *wālid.* The interpretation of these two terms is decisive in the legal debate. Thus it is extremely important to fix their exact linguistic meaning and the interpretation made by jurists.

Walad: *male and female descendants of any degree*

As for the term *walad,* there is no doubt about its meaning from the linguistic point of view, on which there is no divergence (*ḫilāf*). It refers to male and female descendants, however low,[2] and corresponds to the

---

[1] *Tafsīr Manār,* IV, 422; VI, 107; *Tafsīr Rāzī,* II, 378.

[2] *Lisān,* III, 467; *Maǧmaʿ,* II, 17, 149; *Tafsīr Manār,* VI, 109, 110; *Tafsīr Ṭabarī,* IX, 430, 443; *Tafsīr Ṭūsī,* III, 408, 409, 411; *Tāǧ,* II, 540. This meaning is given by Lane (VIII, 2966): ". . . sing. and pl. and masc. and fem.: a child, son, daughter, youngling, or young one; and children, sons, daughters,

Latin *proles.* All law schools use the word *ibn* for male offspring and *bint* or *ibna* for female offspring, if they want to specify the sex of children. Thus, *walad* has a more inclusive sense, as male and female descendants, however low. However, with reference to Qur᾿ān 4:12, Sunnīs, Zaydīs, Ẓāhirīs, and Ibāḍīs limit the meaning of the term only to male descendants of any degree, to daughters, and to female descendants of male children of any degree; while, with reference to Qur᾿ān 4:176, they do not include daughters and male descendants' daughters in the concept of *walad.* In accordance with the linguistic meaning, Ismāᶜīlīs and Imāmīs understand *walad* in the inclusive sense, such that *awlād,* be they male (*ibn*) or female (*ibna, bint*), and *walad al-awlād,* however low, be they male or female, be they either *awlād al-ibn* (*ibn* or *bint al-ibn*) or *awlād al-bint* (*ibn* or *bint al-ibna*), preclude full or consanguine or uterine brothers and sisters from inheritance.[3] It is clear that the difference between the various law schools concerns the inclusion of the *awlād al-bint* in the concept of *walad.* Ismāᶜīlīs and Imāmīs can easily demonstrate that they must be considered as *walad.*[4] In fact, *walad al-walad* takes the place of *walad* if he is not present: *walad al-ibn* takes the place of an *ibn,* while *walad al-bint* takes the place of a *bint.*

The Sunnī reasoning that *walad al-bint* is from a progeny of a different kin is contradicted by the fact that Sunnīs themselves, in one place, interpret *walad* only as a male child with reference to the full sisters (Qur᾿ān 4:176), thus admitting the doctrine of the *ᶜaṣaba maᶜa ġayrihi;* while in another place, *walad* means male and female descendants with reference to husband and wife (Qur᾿ān 4:12). Moreover, Sunnīs contradict themselves in other circumstances too. Thus, according to them, it is not permitted for the *walad al-bint* to marry the wife of his maternal grandfather on the basis of Qur᾿ān 4:22, or for the grandfather to marry the wife of his daughter's son (*ibn bintihi*) on the basis of Qur᾿ān 4:23. Nor it is permitted for a man to testify against his maternal grandfather, because he is considered as an *ibn,* or for a man's maternal grandfather to testify against him, because he is considered as an *ab.* For Sunnīs, *ibn al-bint* is considered as *walad* in all these cases, but not in inheritance.[5] The obvious conclusion is that only Ismāᶜīlīs and Imāmīs interpreted the term *walad* in accordance with its linguistic definition.

---

offspring, young, or younglings; of any kind."

[3] *Ḫilāf,* II, 263, *mas᾿ala*s 25–26; 264, *mas᾿ala* 27; *Tahḏīb Ṭūsī,* IX, 289–90; 316–17, nos. 1136–39; 317–18, no. 1141.

[4] *Ḫilāf,* II, 263, *mas᾿ala* 25; 264, *mas᾿ala* 27.

[5] *Daᶜā᾿im,* II, 366–69, nos. 1331–32; *Ḫilāf,* II, 270–71, *mas᾿ala* 57.

Wālid: *father and any other male ascendant in the paternal line*

The term *wālid* is taken to mean "father" or "mother," while the feminine *wālida* means "mother" only. *Al-wālidān* means "father and mother."[6] However Ismāʿīlīs and Imāmīs do not base themselves on this weak linguistic support, because both Šīʿī schools stress the term *wālidān*[7] and not the implication of the term *wālid,* and because their juridical proof makes reference only to the Qurʾān. In fact, they consider the mother like the father because, according to al-Kulaynī,[8] 1) father and mother are directly related to the deceased, while brothers and sisters are connected to the deceased person through them; 2) father and mother receive an equal share inheriting together with the *walad;* 3) father and mother are never excluded from inheritance. Besides the argument based on the direct relation between the mother and the deceased,[9] Ibn Bābawayh[10] refers to the opinion of al-Faḍl b. Šāḏān[11] (d. 260/874) on the word *wālid.* To the objection that one uses the masculine word *wālid,* not *wālidān* or *wālida,* al-Faḍl answered that, as male and female children are included in the term *walad,* likewise the mother can be called either *wālid* or *ab,* if she inherits together with the father, as Qurʾān 4:11 states: "To each parent (*li-abawayhi*) one-sixth. . . ." Here, one of the *abawān* is the mother, who is called *ab* in the presence of the father; and Qurʾān 2:180 states: "The *waṣiyya* is due to the parents (*liʾl-wālidayn*) and kin"; here too one of the *wālidān* is the mother.

Al-Ṭūsī[12] goes further, stating that in *Sūra* 4:176 (". . . if there is no *walad"*) *walad* can be understood also as the parents because the verse allots the whole estate of a sister to her brother if there is no *walad.* Now, it is well known that the brother does not inherit in the presence of the parents. It is as if Allāh had said: "If a person has died leaving neither *walad* nor *wālidān,* but he has collaterals." Recourse to such a bold interpretation as this notwithstanding, the *iǧmāʿ* of the Imāmī school was

---

[6] *Lisān,* III, 467; *Tāǧ,* II, 541. These meanings are given in Lane (VIII, 2967): ". . . A woman, and any pregnant animal, having a child or young one, or children or young; and bringing forth. Also *wālid* a father and a mother as also *wālida* [which latter is the more common in this use] . . . ; the dual *wālidān* signifies the two parents, the father and the mother."

[7] They often use *wālidān* instead of *wālid* (*Uṣūl Kulaynī,* VII, 71).

[8] Ibid., 71, 74.

[9] *Kitāb man,* IV, 198.

[10] *ʿIlal,* 569–70; *Kitāb man,* IV, 189.

[11] *GAL,* I, 199, S, III, 1201; *GAS,* I, 537–38.

[12] *Ḫilāf,* II, 263.

also based on some Sunnī traditions, like the one reported on the authority of Abū Bakr ("They are *kalāla* if the deceased died leaving neither *walad* nor *wālid"*), or on the authority of ᶜUmar ("I am ashamed because I diverged from Abū Bakr about *kalāla"*), or something similar on the authority of ᶜAlī.

The conclusion is that only the Iraqi law school, and later the Ḥanafīs, Ẓāhirīs, and Ibāḍīs, who interpreted *wālid* as father (and, by analogy, as all male ascendants in the paternal line, however high; cf. *ğadd ṣaḥīḥ,* a true grandfather), respected the true meaning of the term. In brief, no juridical school kept the right meaning of both of the terms *walad* and *wālid.*

Translation of Qurʾān 4:12 and 4:176

In view of the above, I propose the following translation of *Sūra* 4:12: ". . . if a man or a woman leaves his/her inheritance to collaterals and he/she has left a [uterine] brother or a [uterine] sister, each one of the two shall have right to one-sixth; but, if they be more than that, they shall be equal sharers in a third part. . . ."

For the translation of *Sūra* 4:176 I propose: "They will ask thee for a legal decision. Say: Allāh gives you a decision about collaterals: if a man has died leaving no offspring, but he has a [full or consanguine] sister, she shall have right to one-half of the estate. If, instead, a [full or consanguine] brother inherits from his sister who has left no offspring, he shall have right to her whole estate. If there be two [or more full or consanguine] sisters, they shall have the right to two-thirds of the estate. But, if there be [full or consanguine] brothers and sisters inheriting together, a male shall have the right to the double share of a female. . . ."

Qurʾānic rules deriving from Sūras *4:12 and 4:176*

What is, then, the rule envisioned by these Qurʾānic verses? Conclusive information about the original meaning of the terms *kalāla* as collaterals, of *walad* as male and/or female descendants of any degree, and of *wālid* as the father and/or a true grandfather, is given by Ibn Ḥazm.[13] According to him, the inheritance of *kalāla* can be based only on an explicit text (*naṣṣ*) or on an *iğmāᶜ* depending on an explicit text. There was an *iğmāᶜ* on the fact that full, as well as consanguine and uterine, brothers/sisters have the right to inherit if there is neither a son and/or a daughter, nor a male and/or female descendant of a male *walad,* however low, nor a father, nor a true *ğadd,* however high.[14] Ibn Ḥazm goes on to

[13] *Muḥallā,* IX, 299.

[14] This only doctrine is repeated in *Marātib,* 98.

state that the consensus on this doctrine was not uninterrupted in the *Umma* as a whole. In fact, the forefathers (*al-salaf*) diverged on whether it dealt with the inheritance of *kalāla* or not. However, he continues, the rule remains binding unless another explicit text makes an exception to it. Ibn Ḥazm ends stating that such a text existed only in the case of the full or consanguine brothers, who have right to inherit as *ᶜaṣaba bi-nafsihi* if one or more daughters are present, and in the case of a full or consanguine sister, who can inherit as *ᶜaṣaba maᶜa ġayrihi* with one or more daughters if, according to the distinctively Ẓāhirī doctrine, there is no male agnate *iure proprio* (*ᶜāṣib ḏakar*).

I conclude that, for a certain period after the Prophet's death, all collaterals were excluded by male as well as female descendants, and by the father and male ascendants in the paternal line. The divergences began soon after, if we can believe the *ḥadīṯ* of Muᶜāḏ. As a matter of fact, the first exception to the Qurᵓānic rule was the doctrine of the *ᶜaṣaba maᶜa ġayrihi,* which may be traced to the second half of the first century H. at the earliest, if we adopt the criterion of the common transmitter.

Then there arose the debate concerning the question of the grandfather. All the evidence indicates that the juridical elaboration began around the end of the first century and the first half of the second century H. in the different centers (Kūfa, Baṣra, Medina, and Mecca) and continued until the doctrine was standardized in the two main schools of that time, the Iraqi and the Medinese, and the local oppositions were absorbed. Later on, the figures of Abū Ḥanīfa and Mālik were recognized as most representative of the debates involved, and by the end of the second century the juridical elaboration was concluded. There does not seem to have been any specific doctrinal contribution of the Šāfiᶜī, Ḥanbalī, Zaydī, Ẓāhirī, and Ḫāriǧī-Ibāḍī schools to these questions.

As regards the Ismāᶜīlīs and Imāmīs, I am inclined to believe that their doctrine was elaborated during the first half of the third century H., because, apart from their *ḥadīṯ* literature, which seems unauthentic to the Šīᶜī authors themselves, the name of al-Faḍl b. Šāḏān (d. 260/874) emerges with reference to the doctrine of the *ᶜaṣaba maᶜa ġayrihi* and to the interpretation of the term *wālid.* Even later, there remained uncertainty in the Imāmī school on some points of detail.

APPENDIX

SUNNĪ *ISNĀDS*

Kalāla

a) Iraqi school

1) al-Šaʿbī → Ǧābir b. Yazīd → Sufyān al-Ṯawrī (*Muṣannaf,* X, 304, no. 19190) → Wakīʿ → etc. (*Tafsīr Ṭabarī,* VIII, 55, no. 8749)

2) al-Šaʿbī → ʿĀṣim b. Sulaymān al-Aḥwal →
- Ibn ʿUyayna (*Muṣannaf,* X, 304, no. 19191) → etc. (*Tafsīr Ṭabarī,* VIII, 54, no. 8747; *Sunan Bayhaqī,* VI, 224)
- Abū Muʿāwiya (*Muṣannaf Ibn a. Šayba,* XI, 415–16, no. 11646)
- Yazīd b. Hārūn (*Musnad Dārimī,* II, 264, no. 2976)
- ʿAlī b. Mushir → etc. (*Tafsīr Ṭabarī,* VIII, 53–54, no. 8745)
- Hušaym → etc. (*Tafsīr Ṭabarī,* VIII, 54, no. 8746)

3) [ʿAmr b. Šuraḥbīl] →
- al-Zuhrī
- Qatāda →
- Abū Isḥāq

→ Maʿmar (*Muṣannaf,* X, 304, no. 19192) → etc. (*Tafsīr Ṭabarī,* VIII, 57, no. 8763–64)

4) al-Ḥakam → Šuʿba →
- Sahl b. Yūsuf (*Muṣannaf Ibn a. Šayba,* XI, 416, no. 11649) → etc. (*Tafsīr Ṭabarī,* VIII, 57–58, no. 8765)
- Muḥammad b. Ǧaʿfar → etc. (*Tafsīr Ṭabarī,* VIII, 57, no. 8761)

5) al-Suddī → Asbāṭ → Aḥmad b. al-Mufaḍḍal → Muḥammad b. al-Ḥusayn (*Tafsīr Ṭabarī,* VIII, 58–59, no. 8766)

6) Muḥammad b. Zayd → Ibn Wahb → Yūnus (*Tafsīr Ṭabarī,* VIII, 57, no. 8762; 60, no. 8769)

b) Medinese school

7) ᶜUqba b. ᶜĀmir al-Ǧuhanī → Marṯad b. ᶜAbd Allāh al-Yazanī Abū ʾl-Ḫayr → Yazīd b. Abī Ḥabīb
- → Saᶜīd b. Abī Ayyūb → ᶜAbd Allāh b. Yazīd (*Muṣannaf Ibn a. Šayba,* XI, 416, no. 11648; *Musnad Dārimī,* II, 264, no. 2977)
- → Ibn Lahīᶜa → etc. (*Tafsīr Ṭabarī,* IX, 442, no. 10890)

8) Zayd b. Aslam → Mālik (*Muwaṭṭaʾ,* III, 113, no. 1122)

9) Maᶜdān b. Abī Ṭalḥa al-Yaᶜmarī → Sālim b. Abī al-Ǧaᶜd al-Ġaṭafānī → Qatāda
- → Hišām (*Musnad Ṭayālisī,* 11, no. 53) → Yaḥyā b. Saᶜīd (*Musnad Ibn Ḥanbal,* I, 27–28)
  - → Muḥ. b. Abī Bakr al-Muqaddamī and Muḥ. b. al-Muṯannā (*Ṣaḥīḥ Muslim,* XI, 56–57)
  - → Ibn Baššār (*Tafsīr Ṭabarī,* IX, 441, no. 10887)
- → Saᶜīd b. Abī ᶜArūba
  - → Ismāᶜīl b. ᶜUlayya (*Musnad Ibn Ḥanbal,* I, 26) → Abū Bakr b. Abī Šayba (*Ṣaḥīḥ Muslim,* XI, 57; *Sunan Ibn Māǧa,* II, 910–11, no. 2726)
    - → Yaᶜqūb (*Tafsīr Ṭabarī,* IX, 440, no. 10884)
  - → Muḥammad b. Ǧaᶜfar (*Musnad Ibn Ḥanbal,* I, 48–49)
  - → ᶜAbd Allāh b. Bakr al-Sahmī → etc. (*Tafsīr Ṭabarī,* IX, 440, no. 10885)
  - → Ibn Abī ᶜAdī → etc. (*Tafsīr Ṭabarī,* IX, 441, no. 10886)
- → Šuᶜba → etc. (*Ṣaḥīḥ Muslim,* XI, 57; *Tafsīr Ṭabarī,* IX, 437, no. 10877; *Sunan Bayhaqī,* VI, 224)
- → Hammām b. Yaḥyā → ᶜAffān (*Musnad Ibn Ḥanbal,* I, 15)

10) Saʿīd b. al-Musayyib → al-Zuhrī → Maʿmar (*Muṣannaf,* X, 301–2, no. 19183) → etc. (*Tafsīr Ṭabarī,* IX, 438, nos. 10878–79)

11) Muḥammad b. Sīrīn
- → Ayyūb → Maʿmar (*Muṣannaf,* X, 304–5, no. 19193) → etc. (*Tafsīr Ṭabarī,* IX, 435, nos. 10874–75)
- → Ibn ʿAwn → Ismāʿīl b. ʿUlayya → etc. (*Tafsīr Ṭabarī,* IX, 435–36, no. 10876)

12) [Murra] → ʿAmr b. Murra
- → Šuʿba (*Musnad Ṭayālisī,* 12, no. 60) → etc. (*Sunan Bayhaqī,* VI, 225)
- → Sufyān al-Ṯawrī (*Muṣannaf,* X, 302, no. 19184) → Wakīʿ
  - → ʿAlī b. Muḥammad → (*Sunan Ibn Māǧa,* II, 911, no. 2727)
  - → Abū Bakr b. Abī Šayba → (*Sunan Ibn Māǧa,* II, 911, no. 2727)
  - → Ibn Wakīʿ (*Tafsīr Ṭabarī,* IX, 438, no. 10880)

13) Muḥammad b. Ṭalḥa b. Yazīd b. al-Rakkāna → ʿAmr b. Dīnār → Ibn Ǧurayǧ and Ibn ʿUyayna (*Muṣannaf,* X, 302, no. 19185)

14) Sumayṭ b. ʿUmayr → ʿImrān b. Ḥadīr
- → Wakīʿ (*Muṣannaf Ibn a. Šayba,* XI, 417, no. 11652) → Ibn Wakīʿ (*Tafsīr Ṭabarī,* VIII, 54–55, no. 8748)
- → Ḥammād → etc. (*Sunan Bayhaqī,* VI, 224)

Abū ʾl-Safar → Mālik b. Miġwal → Abū Aḥmad al-Zubayr → ʿAmr al-Nāqid (*Ṣaḥīḥ Muslim,* XI, 59)

Abū ʾl-Safar → Mālik b. Miġwal → ʿAbd al-Ṣamad b. al-Nuʿmān → Muḥammad b. Ḫalaf (*Tafsīr Ṭabarī,* IX, 434, no. 10872)

15) al-Barāʾ b. ʿĀzib → Abū Isḥāq →

ʿAmmār b. al-Ruzayq → Yaḥyā b. Ādam (*Musnad Ibn Ḥanbal,* IV, 293) → Abū Kurayb (*Ṣaḥīḥ Muslim,* XI, 59)

Abū Bakr → Yaḥyā b. Ādam

Abū Bakr → Manṣūr b. Abī Muzāḥim (*Sunan Siǧistānī,* III, 79–80, no. 2889; *Sunan Bayhaqī,* VI, 224)

al-Ḥaǧǧāǧ → Maʿmar b. Sulaymān al-Raqqī (*Musnad Ibn Ḥanbal,* IV, 295, 301)

Isrāʾīl → ʿUbayd Allāh b. Mūsā (*Ṣaḥīḥ Buḫārī,* XXIII, 166)

Isrāʾīl → Muṣʿab b. al-Miqdām → etc. (*Tafsīr Ṭabarī,* IX, 434, no. 10873)

Zakariyāʾ → Īsā b. Yūnus → Isḥāq b. Ibrāhīm al-Ḥanṭalī (*Ṣaḥīḥ Muslim.* XI, 59)

Šuʿba → Muḥammad b. Ǧaʿfar → Muḥammad b. al-Muṯannā and Ibn Baššār (*Ṣaḥīḥ Muslim,* XI, 58)

Šuʿba → Muslim b. Ibrāhīm (*Sunan Siǧistānī,* III, 79, no. 2888)

Ismāʿīl b. Abī Ḫālid → Wakīʿ → ʿAlī b. Ḫašram (*Ṣaḥīḥ Muslim,* XI, 58)

Ismāʿīl b. Abī Ḫālid → Wakīʿ → ʿAbd al-Raḥmān b. Bišr → etc. (*Sunan Bayhaqī,* VI, 224)

al-Ḥusayn b. Wāqid → etc. (*Tafsīr Ṭabarī,* IX, 433, no. 10870)

Ibn Abī Ḫālid → etc. (*Tafsīr Ṭabarī,* IX, 434, no. 10871)

c) Meccan school

16) Ṭāwūs → Ibn Ṭāwūs → Maᶜmar (*Muṣannaf,* X, 302–3, no. 19186)

17) Ṭāwūs → Ibn Ṭāwūs → Ibn Ǧurayǧ (*Muṣannaf,* X, 303, no. 19187)

18) Ṭāwūs → Sulaymān al-Aḥwal → Ibn ᶜUyayna (*Muṣannaf,* X, 303, no. 19188; *Muṣannaf Ibn a. Šayba,* XI, 415, no. 11645) →
- Ibn Wakīᶜ (*Tafsīr Ṭabarī,* VIII, 59, no. 8767)
- Saᶜdān b. Naṣr → etc. (*S. Bayhaqī,* VI, 225)

19) Ṭāwūs →
- ᶜAmr b. Dīnār → Ibn ᶜUyayna (*Muṣannaf,* X, 305, no. 19194)
- Ibn Ṭāwūs → Maᶜmar (*Muṣannaf,* X, 305, no. 19195)

20) al-Ḥasan b. Muḥammad b. ᶜAlī b. al-Ḥanafiyya → ᶜAmr b. Dīnār →
- Ibn Ǧurayǧ (*Muṣannaf,* X, 303, no. 19189) →
  - Muḥammad b. Bakr (*Muṣannaf Ibn a. Šayba,* XI, 416, no. 11647)
  - Ibn Wahb → Yūnus (*Tafsīr Ṭabarī,* VIII, 55, no. 8751)
- Ibn ᶜUyayna (*Muṣannaf,* X, 303, no. 19189) →
  - Muḥammad b. Yūsuf (*Musnad Dārimī,* II, 264, no. 2978)
  - Yūnus (*Tafsīr Ṭabarī,* VIII, 45, no. 8735; 55, no. 8750)
  - Muᵓmil → etc. (*Tafsīr Ṭabarī,* VIII, 55, no. 8752)
  - Muḥammad b. Ṣabbāḥ → etc. (*Sunan Bayhaqī,* VI, 225)
  - Saᶜdān b. Naṣr → etc. (*Sunan Bayhaqī,* VI, 225)

21) Salīm b. ᶜAbd al-Salūlī → Abū Isḥāq →
- Isrā'īl → Wakīᶜ (*Muṣannaf Ibn a. Šayba,* XI, 417, no. 11651) → etc. (*Sunan Bayhaqī,* VI, 224)
- Isrā'īl → Yaḥyā b. Ādam → etc. (*Tafsīr Ṭabarī,* VIII, 55–56, nos. 8753–54; 59, no. 8768)
- Abū 'l-Aḥwaṣ → etc. (*Tafsīr Ṭabarī,* VIII, 56, no. 8756)
- Šarīk → etc. (*Tafsīr Ṭabarī,* VIII, 56, no. 8757)
- Sufyān → etc. (*Tafsīr Ṭabarī,* VIII, 56, no. 8758)
- Ašᶜaṯ → etc. (*Tafsīr Ṭabarī,* VIII, 56–57, no. 8759)
- Zakariyā' b. Abī Zā'ida → Hušaym → etc. (*Sunan Bayhaqī,* VI, 224)

ᶜ*Aṣaba maᶜa ġayrihi*

22) al-Aswad b. Yazīd →
- al-Ašᶜaṯ b. Abī 'l-Šaᶜṯā' → Abū Muᶜāwiya Šaybān → etc. (*Ṣaḥīḥ Buḫārī,* XXIII, 161)
- al-Ašᶜaṯ b. Abī 'l-Šaᶜṯā' → Šuᶜba → etc. (*Sunan Bayhaqī,* VI, 233)
- al-Ašᶜaṯ b. Abī 'l-Šaᶜṯā' → Sufyān al-Ṯawrī (*Muṣannaf,* X, 255, no. 19025) → etc. (*Frühislamisches,* 38)
  - Sufyān al-Ṯawrī → Muḥammad b. Yūsuf (*Musnad Dārimī,* II, 250, no. 2882)
  - Sufyān al-Ṯawrī → Wakīᶜ (*Muṣannaf Ibn a. Šayba,* XI, 243, nos. 11115–16)
- Ibrāhīm al-Naḫaᶜī → al-Aᶜmaš → Wakīᶜ (*Muṣannaf Ibn a. Šayba,* XI, 243, nos. 11115–16)
- Ibrāhīm al-Naḫaᶜī → al-Aᶜmaš → Sufyān → etc. (*Frühislamisches,* 38)
- Ibrāhīm al-Naḫaᶜī → Sulaymān → Šuᶜba → etc. (*Ṣaḥīḥ Buḫārī,* XXIII, 165; *Sunan Bayhaqī,* VI, 233)
- Abū Hišām → Qatāda → Abān → etc. (*Sunan Siǧistānī,* III, 80, no. 2893)
- Abū Ḥassān al-Aᶜraǧ → Qatāda → Hišām → Muᶜāḏ b. Hišām → etc. (*Sunan Dāraquṭnī,* IV, 83, no. 50)
- al-Musayyib b. Rāfiᶜ → Yaḥyā b. Ṭalḥa al-Taymī → etc. (*Sunan Dāraquṭnī,* IV, 82–83, no. 48)

23) [al-Aswad b. Yazīd] → Muḥammad b. Sīrīn → Ayyūb → Maᶜmar (*Muṣannaf,* X, 256, no. 19026; 261, no. 19040)

a) Iraqi school

24) ᶜAbd Allāh b. ᶜUtba → Abū Ḥaṣīn → Sufyān al-Ṯawrī → Muᶜāwiya b. Hišām (*Muṣannaf Ibn a. Šayba,* XI, 244, no. 11120)

25) al-Šaᶜbī → Ǧābir → Isrāʾīl → Wakīᶜ (*Muṣannaf Ibn a. Šayba,* XI, 245, no. 11122)

b) Medinese school

26) Abū Salama b. ᶜAbd al-Raḥmān b. ᶜAwf → Yazīd b. Abī Ḥabīb → Yaḥyā b. Ayyūb
→ Zayd b. Ḥabbāb (*Muṣannaf Ibn a. Šayba,* XI, 244, no. 11119)
→ Ibn Wahb → etc. (*Sunan Dāraquṭnī,* IV, 83, no. 49)

27) Ibn Abī ʾl-Zinād → Bišr b. ᶜUmar (*Musnad Dārimī,* II, 251, no. 2884)

28) Ḫāriǧa b. Zayd → Abū ʾl-Zinād → Ibn Abī ʾl-Zinād → Bišr b. ᶜUmar (*Musnad Dārimī,* II, 251, no. 2884)

c) Meccan school

29) Abū Salama b. ᶜAbd al-Raḥmān b. ᶜAwf → al-Zuhrī → Maᶜmar (*Muṣannaf,* X, 254–55, no. 19023) → etc. (*Sunan Bayhaqī,* VI, 233)

30) Ibn Ǧurayǧ (*Muṣannaf,* X, 260, no. 19038)

31) al-Aswad b. Yazīd →
- [Wabra b. ᶜAbd al-Raḥmān] → Ibrāhīm al-Naḫaᶜī → al-Aᶜmaš
  - → Wakīᶜ (*Muṣannaf Ibn a. Šayba,* XI, 243–44, nos. 11117–18)
  - → Sufyān → etc. (*Musnad Dārimī,* II, 251, no. 2883)
- Muḥammad b. Sīrīn → Ayyūb → Ismāᶜīl b. ᶜUlayya (*Muṣannaf Ibn a. Šayba,* XI, 244, no. 11121)
- → al-Ašᶜaṯ b. Abī ᵓl-Šaᶜṯāᵓ → Sufyān al-Ṯawrī → Yazīd b. Hārūn → etc. (*Sunan Bayhaqī,* VI, 233)

32) al-Musayyib b. Rāfiᶜ → ᶜAlī b. Mushir (*Muṣannaf Ibn a. Šayba,* XI, 245, no. 11123)

33) Huzayl b. Šuraḥbīl al-Awdī → Abū Qays al-Awdī → Šuᶜba (*Musnad Ṭayālisī,* 49, no. 375) → etc. (*Musnad Ibn Ḥanbal,* I, 463–64; *Ṣaḥīḥ Buḫārī,* XXIII, 162; *Sunan Tirmiḏī,* III, 281; *Sunan Bayhaqī,* VI, 229, 233)
- → al-Ḥaǧǧāǧ b. Arṭāh
  - → Abū Ḫālid al-Aḥmar (*Muṣannaf Ibn a. Šayba,* XI, 246, no. 11125)
  - → Ḥammād b. Salama → etc. (*Sunan Dāraquṭnī,* IV, 80, no. 41)
- → Sufyān al-Ṯawrī (*Muṣannaf,* X, 257, nos. 19031–32) → etc. (*Frühislamisches,* 37)
  - → Wakīᶜ (*Muṣannaf Ibn a. Šayba,* XI, 245–46, no. 11124; *Musnad Ibn Ḥanbal,* I, 389) → etc. (*Sunan Ibn Māǧa,* II, 909, no. 2721; *Sunan Dāraquṭnī,* IV, 80, no. 39)
  - → Muḥammad b. Yūsuf (*Musnad Dārimī,* II, 252, no. 2893) → etc. (*Sun. Dāraq.*, IV, 80, no. 40)
  - → ᶜAbd al-Raḥmān (*Musnad Ibn Ḥanbal,* I, 440) → etc. (*Ṣaḥīḥ Buḫārī,* XXIII, 165; *Sunan Bayhaqī,* VI, 230)
  - → Yazīd b. Hārūn → etc. (*Sunan Tirmiḏī,* III, 280–81; *Sunan Dāraquṭnī,* IV, 79–80, no. 38; *Sunan Bayhaqī,* VI, 230)
  - → Qabīṣa and ᶜUbayd Allāh b. Mūsā → etc. (*Sunan Bayhaqī,* VI, 230)
- → Ibn Abī Laylā → Hušaym (*Musnad Ibn Ḥanbal,* I, 428)
- → al-Aᶜmaš → ᶜAlī b. Mushir → etc. (*Sunan Siǧistānī,* III, 80, no. 2890)

IMĀMĪ *ISNĀDS*

34) Abū Ǧaᶜfar → Muḥ. b. Muslim → Abū Ayyūb al-Ḫazzār → al-Ḥasan b. Maḥbūb ↗ Sahl b. Ziyād → etc. (*Uṣūl Kulaynī,* VII, 82–83, no. 1; *Ṣaḥīḥ,* III, 263, no. 3920)

al-Ḥasan b. Maḥbūb ↘ [Ibrāhīm] → Aḥmad b. Muḥammad b. ᶜĪsā (*Tahḏīb Ṭūsī,* IX, 319, no. 1145) and ᶜAlī b. Ibrāhīm → etc. (*Uṣūl Kul.,* VII, 83; 99, no. 1; *Ṣaḥīḥ,* III, 263, no. 3921; 274, no. 3953)

Zurāra → Ǧamīl b. Darrāǧ → Aḥmad b. Muḥammad b. Abī Naṣr ↗ [Ibrāhīm]

35) Zurāra → ᶜAlī b. Saᶜīd → Mūsā b. Bakr → Ṣafwān → al-Ḥasan b. Muḥammad b. Samāᶜa (*Tahḏīb Ṭūsī,* IX, 288–89, no. 1043) → Ḥumayd b. Ziyād (*Uṣūl Kulaynī,* VII, 97, no. 3)

36) Abū ᶜAbd Allāh → Ḥamza b. Ḥumrān → ᶜAlī b. Ribāṭ → al-Ḥasan b. Muḥammad b. Samāᶜa (*Tahḏīb Ṭūsī,* IX, 319, no. 1146) → etc. (*Uṣūl Kulaynī,* VII, 99, no. 2; *Ṣaḥīḥ,* III, 274, no. 3954)

37) Abū ᶜAbd Allāh ↗ some Companions ↘ Muḥammad b. Abī ᶜUmayr

Abū ᶜAbd Allāh ↘ ᶜAbd al-Raḥmān b. al-Ḥaǧǧāǧ ↗ Muḥammad b. Abī ᶜUmayr

Muḥammad b. Abī ᶜUmayr ↗ Yaᶜqūb b. Yazīd → Saᶜd b. ᶜAbd Allāh → etc. (*Maᶜānī,* 258)

Muḥammad b. Abī ᶜUmayr ↘ al-Faḍl b. Šāḏān (*Tahḏīb Ṭūsī,* IX, 319, no. 1147) → etc. (*Uṣūl Kulaynī,* VII, 99, no. 3; *Ṣaḥīḥ,* III, 274, no. 3955)

38) al-Riḍā → Muḥammad b. Ismāᶜīl b. Bazīᶜ → Aḥmad b. Muḥammad b. ᶜĪsā (*Musnad Riḍā,* II, 432, no. 4; *Tahḏīb Ṭūsī,* IX, 323–24, no. 1161)

39) Abū ᶜAbd Allāh → Zurāra → Muṯannā al-Ḥannāṭ → al-Ḥasan b. ᶜAlī al-Ḫazzāz and ᶜAlī b. al-Ḥakam → Aḥmad b. Muḥammad b. ᶜĪsā (*Istibṣār,* IV, 146–47, nos. 549–51; *Tahḏīb Ṭūsī,* IX, 293, no. 1049; 320–21, nos. 1149–52)

40) Abū ᶜAbd Allāh → Faḍīl b. Yasār → ᶜAlī b. Riṯāb ↘
Abū Ǧaᶜfar → Abū Baṣīr → Ḥammād ↗ al-Ḥasan b. Maḥbūb → al-Ḥasan b. Muḥammad b. Samāᶜa (*Istibṣār*, IV, 161, nos. 611–12)

41) Zurāra → Ḥarīz → ᶜAbd Allāh b. Baḥr → al-Ḥusayn b. Saᶜīd → Aḥmad b. Muḥammad b. Īsā (*Tahḏīb Ṭūsī*, IX, 280–81. no. 1014) → etc. (*Uṣūl Kulaynī*, VII, 93, no. 7; *Ṣaḥīḥ*, III, 268–69, no. 3942)

42) ᶜUbayd b. Zurāra → ᶜAbd Allāh b. Bakīr → Ibn Faḍḍāl → Aḥmad b. Muḥammad b. ᶜĪsā (*Tahḏīb Ṭūsī*, IX, 281–82. no. 1018)

43) Zurāra → ᶜAlī b. Saᶜīd → Mūsā b. Bakr → Fuḍāla b. Ayyūb → al-Ḥusayn b. Saᶜīd → Aḥmad b. Muḥammad b. Īsā (*Uṣūl Kulaynī*, VII, 104)

44) Zurāra → ᶜUmar b. Uḏayna → Yūnus → Muḥammad b. Abī ᶜUmayr and Muḥammad b. ᶜĪsā → Ibrāhīm → ᶜAlī b. Ibrāhīm (*Uṣūl Kulaynī*, VII, 91–92, no. 1; *Ṣaḥīḥ*, III, 267, no. 3936; *Tahḏīb Ṭūsī*, IX, 280, no. 1013)

45) Zurāra → ᶜUmar b. Uḏayna → Muḥammad b. Abī ᶜUmayr → Ibrāhīm → ᶜAlī b. Ibrāhīm (*Uṣūl Kulaynī*, VII, 100–101)

46) ᶜAbd Allāh b. Muḥriz → ᶜUmar b. Uḏayna → Muḥammad b. Abī ᶜUmayr → Ibrāhīm → ᶜAlī b. Ibrāhīm (*Uṣūl Kulaynī*, VII, 100, no. 2)

LIST OF ABBREVIATIONS

Aġānī = Abū ᵓl-Farağ al-Iṣfahānī (d. 356/967), *Kitāb al-Aġānī.*

Aḥkām = al-Šāfiᶜī (d. 204/820), *Aḥkām al-Qurᵓān.*

Aḥkām Qurᵓān = Ibn al-ᶜArabī (d. 543/1148), *Aḥkām al-Qurᵓān.*

Aᶜlām = al-Ziriklī, Ḫayr al-Dīn, *al-Aᶜlām.*

Aᶜšā = H. Thorbecke, "Al-Aᶜšâ's Lobgedichte auf Muḥammad."

Āṯār = Abū Yūsuf (d. 182/798), *Kitāb al-Āṯār.*

Āṯār Nuᶜmān = al-Nuᶜmān b. Muḥammad (d. 363/974), *Muḫtaṣar al-āṯār fi-mā ruwiya ᶜan al-aᵓimma al-aṭhār,* MS.

Aᶜyān = al-Amīn, Muḥsin (d. 1371/1952), *Aᶜyān al-Šīᶜa.*

ᶜAyn = al-Ḫalīl b. Aḥmad (d. 175/791), *Kitāb al-ᶜAyn.*

Baḥr = Ibn al-Murtaḍā (d. 840/1437), *Kitāb al-Baḥr al-zaḫḫār al-ğāmiᶜ li-maḏāhib ᶜulamāᵓ al-amṣār.*

Carmen Aᶜšā = M. F. Brag and T. Thorelius, *Carmen Ashae* . . . .

Concordance = A. J. Wensinck, *Concordance et indices de la tradition musulmane.*

Corpus = Zayd ibn ᶜAlī, *"Corpus Juris".*

Daᶜāᵓim = al-Nuᶜmān b. Muḥammad, *Daᶜāᵓim al-Islām.*

Dir. ered. I = Agostino Cilardo, *Diritto ereditario islamico delle scuole giuridiche ismailita e imamita: Casistica.*

Dir. ered. II = Agostino. Cilardo, *Diritto ereditario islamico delle scuole giuridiche sunnite (ḥanafita, mālikita, šāfiᶜita e ḥanbalita) e delle scuole giuridiche zaydita, ẓāhirita e ibāḍita: Casistica.*

Diritto = al-Basīwī (d. V/XI c.), *al-Muḫtaṣar.*

Divan Farazdak = Joseph Hell, *Divan des Farazdak,* photolith. Wiedergabe.

Divan Férazdak = Farazdaq (d. ca. 110/728), *Divan de Férazdak* (ed. and trans. R. Boucher).

Dīwān Aᶜšā = R. Geyer, *Gedichte von 'Abû Baṣîr Maimûn Ibn Qays al-'A'šâ . . . und von Al-Musayyab Ibn 'Alas.*

Dīwān Farazdaq = *Dīwān al-Farazdaq,* Beirut 1380/1960.

Dīwāns = Charles Lyall, *The Dīwāns of ᶜAbīd Ibn al-Abraṣ, of Asad, ᶜĀmir Ibn aṭ-Ṭufail, of ᶜĀmir Ibn Ṣaᶜṣaᶜah.*

Durr = al-Suyūṭī (d. 911/1505), *al-Durr al-naṯīr* (on margin of *Nihāya,* q.v.).

EI = *First Encyclopaedia of Islam.*

EI² = *Encyclopaedia of Islam* (2d edition).

Farāᵓiḍ = Abū Ḥanīfa (d. 150/767), *Risālat al-farāᵓiḍ.*

Fatāwā = al-Subkī (d. 756/1355), *Fatāwā al-Subkī.*
Fihrist = Ibn al-Nadīm (d. 385/995), *Kitāb al-Fihrist,* ed. Flügel.
Fihrist Ṭūsī = al-Ṭūsī (d. 460/1067), *al-Fihrist* or *Fihrist kutub al-Šīʿa.*
Fiqh = al-Ǧubūrī, *Fiqh al-imām al-Awzāʿī.*
Frühislamisches = Sufyān al-Ṯawrī (d. 161/778), "Frühislamisches Erbrecht nach dem *Kitāb al-Farāʾiḍ* des Sufyān al-Thawrī."
GAL = Carl Brockelmann, *Geschichte der arabischen Litteratur.*
Ǧamhara = Ibn Durayd (d. 321/933), *Ǧamharat al-luġa.*
Ǧāmiʿ = Ibn Wahb (d. 197/812), *Le Djâmi' d'Ibn Wahb.*
Ǧāmiʿ Ibn Baraka = Ibn Baraka (d. V/XI c.), *Kitāb al-Ǧāmiʿ.*
Ǧāmiʿ kabīr = al-Šaybānī (d. 189/805), *al-Ǧāmiʿ al-kabīr.*
Ǧarḥ = Ibn Abī Ḥātim (d. 327/938), *Kitāb al-Ǧarḥ waʾl-taʿdīl.*
GAS = F. Sezgin, *Geschichte des arabischen Schrifttums.*
Guillaume = A. Guillaume, *The Life of Muhammad:* A Translation of Ibn Isḥāq's *Sīrat Rasūl Allāh,* Oxford 1955.
Hidāya = Ibn Bābawayh (d. 381/991), *al-Muqniʿ waʾl-Hidāya.*
Ḫilāf = al-Ṭūsī, *Kitāb al-Ḫilāf.*
Ḫizāna = Abū ʾl-Layṯ al-Samarqandī (d. 373/983), *Ḫizānat al-fiqh wa-ʿuyūn al-masāʾil.*
Howell = Mortimer Sloper Howell, *Grammar of the Classical Arabic Language. . . .*
Ḥuffāẓ = al-Suyūṭī (d. 911/1505), *Ṭabaqāt al-ḥuffāẓ.*
Ḥuǧǧa = al-Šaybānī, *al-Ḥuǧǧa fī iḫtilāf ahl al-Kūfa wa-ahl al-Madīna,* MS.
Ḫulāṣa = al-Fattānī, *Ḫulāṣat al-Farāʾiḍ.*
Iḥkām = Ibn Ḥazm (d. 456/1064), *al-Iḥkām fī uṣūl al-aḥkām.*
Iḫtilāf = al-Šāfiʿī (d. 204/820), *Kitāb Iḫtilāf al-ḥadīṯ.*
Iḫtilāf Ṭaḥāwī = al-Ṭaḥāwī (d. 321/933), *Iḫtilāf al-fuqahāʾ.*
ʿIlal = Ibn Bābawayh, *ʿIlal al-šarāʾiʿ.*
Iqtiṣār = al-Nuʿmān b. Muḥammad, *Kitāb al-Iqtiṣār.*
Iršād = Yāqūt (d. 626/1229), *Iršād al-arīb ilā maʿrifat al-adīb.*
Isʿāf = al-Suyūṭī, *Kitāb Isʿāf al-mubaṭṭaʾ bi-riǧāl al-Muwaṭṭaʾ.*
Istibṣār = al-Tūsī, *al-Istibṣār fī-mā iḫtalafa min al-aḫbār.*
Kāfī = Ibn Qudāma (d. 620/1223), *al-Kāfī fī fiqh al-imām Aḥmad b. Ḥanbal.*
Kifāya = al-Ǧurǧānī (d. 482/1089), *Kitāb al-Kifāya fī maʿrifat al-farāʾiḍ wa-qismat al-mawārīṯ,* MS.
Kitāb man = Ibn Bābawayh, *Kitāb man lā yaḥḍuruhu ʾl-faqīh.*
Leben = Joseph Hell, *Das Leben des Farazdak nach seinen Gedichten und sein Loblied auf al-Walîd ibn Jazîd.*

Leben Mohammed = Ibn Hišām, *Das Leben Mohammed's* nach Mohammed Ibn Ishak bearbeitet von Abd el-Malik Ibn Hischam, aus dem Arabischen übersetzt von Gustav Weil.
Lexicon = Edward William Lane, *An Arabic-English Lexicon.*
Lisān = Ibn Manẓūr (d. 711/1311), *Lisān al-ᶜArab.*
Littérature = Carlo Alfonso Nallino, *La littérature arabe des origines à l'époque de la dynastie umayyade.*
Maᶜānī = Ibn Bābawayh, *Maᶜānī al-aḫbār.*
Mabsūṭ = al-Saraḫsī (d. 483/1090), *Kitāb al-Mabsūṭ.*
Maǧmaᶜ = al-Ṭabarsī (d. 548/1153), *Maǧmaᶜ al-Bayān.*
Marātib = Ibn Ḥazm, *Marātib al-igmāᶜ.*
Masāᵓil = Abū Dāwūd al-Siǧistānī (d. 275/888), *Kitāb Masāᵓil al-imām Aḥmad b. Ḥanbal.*
Masāᵓil Dāwūd = al-Šaṭṭī (d. 1379/1959), *Risāla fī Masāᵓil al-imām Dāwūd al-Ẓāhirī.*
Minhāǧ = al-Nawawī (d. 676/1278), *Minhâdj aṭ-Ṭâlibîn.*
Minhāǧ Nuᶜmān = al-Nuᶜmān b. Muḥammad, *Minhāǧ al-farāᵓiḍ,* MS (cf. *GAS*, I, 578, no. 22).
Mudawwana = Mālik b. Anas (d. 179/795), *al-Mudawwana al-kubrā, riwāyat al-Imām Saḥnūn b. Saᶜīd al-Tanūḫī* (d. 240/854).
Mudawwana kubrā = al-Ḫurāsānī al-Ibāḍī, Abū Ġānim Bišr b. Ġānim (d. ca. 200/815), *al-Mudawwana al-kubrā.*
Muġnī = Ibn Qudāma, *al-Muġnī.*
Muḥallā = Ibn Ḥazm, *Kitāb al-Muḥallā.*
Muḥkam = Ibn Sīda (d. 458/1066), *Kitāb al-Muḥkam waᵓl-muḥīṭ al-aᶜẓam fī ᵓl-luġa.*
Muḫtaṣar Basīwī = al-Basīwī, *al-Muḫtaṣar;* cf. *Diritto.*
Muḫtaṣar Ḫalīl = Ḫalīl b. Isḥāq (d. 776/1374), *al-Muḫtaṣar,* trans. I. Guidi and D. Santillana, *Il "Mukhtaṣar" o Sommario del diritto malechita.*
Muḫtaṣar Ḫiraqī = al-Ḫiraqī (d. 334/945–46), *al-Muḫtaṣar.*
Muḫtaṣar Ibrāhīm = Ibn Qays, Abū Isḥāq Ibrāhīm (d. 475/1082), *Muḫtaṣar al-Ḫiṣāl.*
Muḫtaṣar Muzanī = al-Muzanī (d. 264/878), *al-Muḫtaṣar.*
Muḫtaṣar Qudūrī = al-Qudūrī (d. 428/1037), *al-Muḫtaṣar.*
Muḫtaṣar Ṭaḥāwī = al-Ṭaḥāwī, *al-Muḫtaṣar.*
Muqniᶜ = Ibn Qudāma, *al-Muqniᶜ fī fiqh imām al-sunna Aḥmad b. Ḥanbal.*
Muqniᶜ Ibn Bābawayh = Ibn Bābawayh, *al-Muqniᶜ waᵓl-Hidāya.*
Muṣannaf = ᶜAbd al-Razzāq (d. 211/826), *al-Muṣannaf.*

Muṣannaf Ibn a. Šayba = Ibn Abī Šayba (d. 235/849), *al-Kitāb al-Muṣannaf fī ᵓl-aḥādīṯ waᵓl-āṯār.*
Muṣannaf Kindī = al-Kindī (d. 557/1162), *al-Muṣannaf.*
Musnad Abī Ḥanīfa = Abū Ḥanīfa, *Musnad al-imām Abī Ḥanīfa.*
Musnad Dārimī = al-Dārimī (d. 255/869), *al-Musnad al-ǧāmiᶜ* or *al-Sunan.*
Musnad Ḥumaydī = al-Ḥumaydī (d. 219/834), *al-Musnad.*
Musnad Ibn Ḥanbal = Ibn Ḥanbal (d. 241/855), *al-Musnad.*
Musnad Riḍā = Ibn Bābawayh al-Qummī, *Musnad al-imām Riḍā.*
Musnad Šāfiᶜī = al-Šāfiᶜī, *Tartīb Musnad al-imām . . . al-Šāfiᶜī.*
Musnad Ṭayālisī = al-Ṭayālisī (d. 203/818–19), *Kitāb al-Musnad.*
Muwaṭṭaᵓ = Mālik b. Anas, *Kitāb al-Muwaṭṭaᵓ,* related by. Yaḥyā b. Yaḥyā al-Layṯī al-Andalusī, with the *šarḥ* by al-Zurqānī.
Muwaṭṭaᵓ Šaybānī = Mālik b. Anas, *Kitāb al-Muwaṭṭaᵓ,* as related by al-Šaybānī.
Nihāya = Ibn al-Aṯīr (d. 606/1210), *al-Nihāya fī ġarīb al-ḥadīṯ waᵓl-aṯar.*
Nīl = al-Muṣᶜabī (d. 1223/1808), *Kitāb al-Nīl wa-šifāᵓ al-ᶜalīl.*
Origins = Joseph Schacht, *The Origins of Muhammadan Jurisprudence.*
Poësis = Ibn Qutayba (d. 276/889), *Liber poësis et poëtarum.*
Powers = David Stephan Powers, *Studies in Qurᵓan and* Ḥadīth: *The Formation of the Islamic Law of Inheritance.*
Qāmūs = al-Fīrūzābādī (d. 817/1415), *al-Qāmūs al-muḥīṭ.*
Recueil = A. Querry, *Recueil de lois concernant les musulmans schyites;* trans. of the *Šarāᵓiᶜ* of al-Muḥaqqiq al-Ḥillī.
Riǧāl = al-Ṭūsī, *Riǧāl al-Ṭūsī.*
Riǧāl Ḥillī = Ibn al-Muṭahhar al-Ḥillī (d. 726/1325), *Riǧāl al-ᶜAllāma al-Ḥillī.*
Riǧāl Kaššī = al-Kaššī (d. 340/951), *Riǧāl al-Kaššī.*
Riǧāl Naǧāšī = al-Naǧāšī (d. 450/1058), *Kitāb al-Riǧāl,* or *Asmāᵓ al-Riǧāl.*
Risāla Qayrawānī = Ibn Abī Zayd al-Qayrawānī (d. 386/996), *La Risâla ou Épitre sur les éléments du dogme et de la loi de l'islam selon le rite mâlikite.*
Risāla Šāfiᶜī¹ = al-Šāfiᶜī, *al-Risāla [al-qadīma].*
Risāla Šāfiᶜī² = al-Šāfiᶜī, *al-Risāla [al-ǧadīda].*
Ṣaḥīḥ = al-Bahbūdī (d. ca. 826/1423), *Ṣaḥīḥ al-Kāfī.*
Ṣaḥīḥ Buḫārī = al-Buḫārī (d. 256/870), *Ṣaḥīḥ,* with the *šarḥ* by al-Kirmānī.
Ṣaḥīḥ Muslim = Muslim (d. 261/875), *Ṣaḥīḥ,* with the *šarḥ* by al-Nawawī.

Šarāʾiᶜ = al-Muḥaqqiq al-Ḥillī (d. 676/1277), *Šarāʾiᶜ al-Islām fī masāʾil al-ḥalāl waʾl-ḥarām.*
Šarḥ Dīwān Farazdaq = al-Ṣāwī, *Šarḥ Dīwān al-Farazdaq.*
Šarḥ Muwaṭṭaʾ = *Šarḥ* by al-Zurqānī (d. 1122/1710) on Mālik b. Anas, *Kitāb al-Muwaṭṭaʾ*, as related by Yaḥyā b. Yaḥyā.
Šarḥ Muwaṭṭaʾ Šaybānī = *Šarḥ* by Muḥammad ᶜAbd al-Ḥayy al-Laknawī (d. 1886 or 7) on Mālik b. Anas, *Kitāb al-Muwaṭṭaʾ*, as related by al-Šaybānī.
Šarḥ Nīl = Aṭfayyiš (d. 1332/1914), *Šarḥ al-Nīl wa-šifāʾ al-ᶜalīl.*
Šarḥ Siyar = al-Saraḫsī, *Šarḥ kitāb al-Siyar al-kabīr,* in *Kitāb al-Siyar al-kabīr,* with the *šarḥ* by al-Saraḫsī.
Sīra = Ibn Hišām (d. 218/834), Das *Leben Muhammed's* nach Muhammed Ibn Ishâk, bearbeitet von Abd el-Malik Ibn Hischâm.
Siyar = al-Šaybānī, *Kitāb al-Siyar al-kabīr;* cf. *Šarḥ Siyar.*
Studies = Agostino Cilardo, *Studies on the Islamic Law of Inheritance.*
Sunan Bayhaqī = al-Bayhaqī (d. 458/1066), *al-Sunan al-kubrā.*
Sunan Dāraquṭnī = al-Dāraquṭnī (d. 385/995), *al-Sunan.*
Sunan Ibn Māǧa = Ibn Māǧa (d. 273/887), *Sunan.*
Sunan Siǧistānī = Abū Dāwūd al-Siǧistānī, *Kitāb al-Sunan.*
Sunan Tirmiḏī = al-Tirmiḏī (d. 279/892), *Kitāb al-Sunan* or *al-Ǧāmiᶜ al-ṣaḥīḥ.*
Sunna = al-Marwazī (d. 294/906), *al-Sunna.*
Ṭabaqāt = Ibn Saᶜd (d. 230/845), *Kitāb al-Ṭabaqāt al-kabīr.*
Ṭabaqāt kubrā = Ibn Saᶜd, *Kitāb al-Ṭabaqāt al-kubrā.*
Tables = Ignazio Guidi, *Tables alphabétiques du Kitâb al-Aġânî.*
Taḏkira = al-Ḏahabī (d. 748/1348), *Kitāb Taḏkirat al-ḥuffāẓ.*
Tafsīr Furāt = Ibn Furāt al-Kūfī (d. 310/922), *Tafsīr Furāt al-Kūfī.*
Tafsīr Manār = Muḥammad ᶜAbduh (d. 1323/1905) and Muḥammad Rašīd Riḍā (d. 1354/1935), *Tafsīr al-Qurʾān al-karīm,* known as *Tafsīr al-Manār.*
Tafsīr Nasafī = al-Nasafī (d. 710/1310), *Tafsīr al-Nasafī.*
Tafsīr Nīsābūrī = al-Nīsābūrī (c. IX/XV), *Tafsīr ġarāʾib al-Qurʾān wa-raġāʾib al-furqān.*
Tafsīr Rāzī = al-Rāzī (d. 606/1209), *Mafātīḥ al-ġayb,* known as *al-Tafsīr al-kabīr.*
Tafsīr Ṭabarī = al-Ṭabarī (d. 310/923), *Ǧāmiᶜ al-Bayān ᶜan al-Qurʾān: Tafsīr al-Ṭabarī.*
Tafsīr Ṯawrī = Sufyān al-Ṯawrī, *Tafsīr al-Qurʾān al-karīm.*
Tafsīr Ṭūsī = al-Ṭūsī, *al-Tibyān fī tafsīr al-Qurʾān.*
Tāǧ = al-Murtaḍā al-Zabīdī (d. 1205/1791), *Tāǧ al-ᶜarūs.*

Tāǧ luġa = al-Ǧawharī (d. 393/1003), *Kitāb Tāǧ al-luġa wa-ṣiḥāḥ al-ᶜarabiyya.*

Tahḏīb = Ibn Ḥaǧar al-ᶜAsqalānī, (d. 852/1449), *Kitāb Tahḏīb al-Tahḏīb.*

Tahḏīb luġa = al-Azharī (d. 370/980), *Tahḏīb al-luġa.*

Tahḏīb Ṭūsī = al-Ṭūsī, *Tahḏīb al-Aḥkām.*

Teorie = Agostino Cilardo, *Teorie sulle origini del diritto islamico.*

Translations = Charles J. Lyall, *Translations of Ancient Arabian Poetry: Chiefly Pre-Islamic.*

Tuḥfa = Ibn ᶜĀṣim (d. 829/1426), *Traité de Droit Musulman: La Tohfat d'Ebn Acem.*

ᶜUmda = Ibn Qudāma, *al-ᶜUmda fī fiqh imām al-sunna Aḥmad b. Ḥanbal al-Šaybānī.*

ᶜUmda Ibn Rašīq = Ibn Rašīq al-Qayrawānī (d. 456/1064), *al-ᶜUmda fī maḥāsin al-šiᶜr wa-ādābihi wa-naqdihi.*

Umm = al-Šāfiᶜī, *Kitāb al-Umm.*

Uṣūl = al-Mutawakkil ᶜalā ᵓllāh Aḥmad b. Sulaymān b. al-Hādī ilā ᵓl-Ḥaqq (d. 566/1170), *Kitāb Uṣūl al-aḥkām fī ᵓl-ḥalāl waᵓl-ḥarām,* MS.

Uṣūl Kulaynī = al-Kulaynī (d. 328/939), *al-Uṣūl min al-Kāfī, al-Furūᶜ min al-Kāfī, al-Rawḍa min al-Kāfī.*

ᶜUyūn = Abū ᵓl-Layṯ al-Samarqandī, *Ḫizānat al-fiqh wa-ᶜuyūn al-masāᵓil.*

Weil = Gustav Weil, *Die poetische Literatur der Araber vor und unmittelbar nach Mohammed: Eine historisch-kritische Skizze.*

BIBLIOGRAPHY

ᶜAbd al-Razzāq b. Hammām al-Ḥimyarī. *Al-Muṣannaf.* 11 vols. Karachi 1390–92/1970–72.

Abdul Qayyum, M. *Indices to the Lisān al-ᶜArab, Index I: Names of Poets.* Lahore 1938.

Abū Dāwūd al-Siǧistānī. *Kitāb al-Sunan.* 4 vols. Beirut 1970.

———. *Kitāb Masāʾil al-imām Aḥmad b. Ḥanbal.* Ed. Muḥammad Rašīd Riḍā. Cairo 1353/1934. Ed. Zuhayr Šāwīš. Beirut 1401/1981.

Abū Dāwūd al-Ṭayālisī. *Kitāb al-Musnad.* See al-Ṭayālisī, Abū Dāwūd Sulaymān b. Dāwūd, *Kitāb al-Musnad.*

Abū Ġānim al-Ḫurāsānī al-Ibāḍī. *Al-Mudawwana al-kubrā.* See al-Ḫurāsānī al-Ibāḍī, Abū Ġānim Bišr b. Ġānim, *al-Mudawwana al-kubrā.*

Abū Ḥanīfa. *Musnad al-imām Abī Ḥanīfa.* Ed. Ṣafwat al-Saqqā. Aleppo 1382/1962.

———. *Risālat al-Farāʾiḍ.* Ed. A. Cilardo, "Un antico documento di diritto ereditario musulmano," in *Annali I.U.O.N.* 42 (1982): 103–26.

Abū ʾl-Farağ al-Iṣfahānī. *Kitāb al-Aġānī.* 20 vols. Būlāq 1285/1868–69.

Abū ʾl-Layṯ al-Samarqandī. *Ḫizānat al-fiqh wa-ᶜUyūn al-masāʾil.* Ed. Ṣalāḥ al-Dīn al-Nāhī. 2 vols. Baghdad 1385–86/1965–67.

Abū Tammām. See Ḥabīb b. Aws, Abū Tammām, al-Ṭāʾī.

Abū Yūsuf Yaᶜqūb b. Ibrāhīm al-Anṣārī. *Kitāb al-Āṯār.* Ed. Abū ʾl-Wafā. Ḥaydarābād 1355/1936.

Abū Zayd Saᶜīd b. Aws al-Anṣārī. *Kitāb al-Hamz.* Traité philologique inédit par Abu Zaïd al-Anṣârî édité par le P. L. Cheikho. Beyrouth 1911.

———. *Kitāb al-Maṭar.* Transcribed from a manuscript in the Bibliothèque Nationale, Paris, and edited, with notes, by R. J. H. Gottheil, 1895. Excerpt from the *Journal of the American Oriental Society,* vol. XVI, pp. 282–317.

———. *Kitāb al-Nawādir fī ʾl-luġa.* Ed. with cmt. al-Ḫūrī al-Šartūnī al-Lubnānī. Beirut 1894.

Aḥmad b. Ḥanbal. See Ibn Ḥanbal, Aḥmad b. Muḥammad.

Āmilī, Muḥsin al-Ḥusaynī. See al-Amīn, Muḥsin.

al-Amīn, Muḥsin (LC lists under Āmilī, Muḥsin al-Ḥusaynī). *Aᶜyān al-Šīᶜa.* 54 vols. Beirut and Damascus 1370–82/1951–62.

ᶜAntara b. Šaddād. *Dīwān.* Beirut 1377/1958.

———. *Dīwān ᶜAntara,* 3rd ed. Beirut 1863.

———. *Kitāb cAntara b. Šaddād.* 6 vols. Beirut 1883–84.

———. *Kitāb Munyat al-nafs fī ašcār cAntar cAbs.* Intiḫāb Iskandar Aġā Abkāriūs. Beirut 1864.

Arkoun, Mohammed. *Lectures du Coran.* Tunis 1991.

Arnold, Fr. Aug. Septem Mucallaḳât Carmina Antiquissima Arabum, Lipsiæ 1850.

Aṭfayyiš (LC: Aṭṭafayyish), Muḥammad b. Yūsuf. *Šarḥ al-Nīl wa-šifāʾ al-calīl.* 10 vols. Cairo 1343/1924–25.

al-Awzācī, cAbd al-Raḥmān b. cAmr. See al-Ǧubūrī, cAbd Allāh Muḥammad, *Fiqh al-imām al-Awzācī.*

al-Azharī, Muḥammad b. Aḥmad. *Tahḏīb al-luġa.* Ed. cAbd al-Salām Muḥammad Hārūn and Muḥammad cAlī al-Naǧǧār. 15 vols. Cairo 1964.

al-Bahbūdī, Muḥammad al-Bāqir. *Ṣaḥīḥ al-Kāfī* (selected *ḥadīṯ*s from *Kitāb al-Kāfī* by al-Kulaynī). 3 vols. Beirut 1401/1981.

al-Bārūdī, Maḥmūd Sāmī. *Dīwān.* 2 vols. Cairo n.d.

al-Basīwī, Abū ʾl-Ḥasan cAlī b. Muḥammad. *Al-Muḫtaṣar.* Zanzibar 1886. Ed. cAbd al-Qādir cAṭā and Muḥammad cAlī Zurqa. cUmān 1397/1977. The chapters on the law of inheritance are translated into German by E. Sachau, "Muhammedanisches Erbrecht nach der Lehre der Ibaditischen Araber von Zanzibar und Ostafrika," in *Sitzungsberichte der K. Preussichen Akademie der Wissenschaften zu Berlin,* VIII, 1894. From German into Italian by I. Guidi, "Il diritto ereditario musulmano secondo la dottrina degli arabi ibaditi di Zanzibar e dell'Africa Orientale," in *Rivista Coloniale,* 1906, pp. 173–96, 335–87.

al-Bayhaqī, Aḥmad b. al-Ḥusayn. *Al-Sunan al-kubrā.* 10 vols. Ḥaydarābād 1354–56/1925–27; reprint, 10 vols. with index, Beirut 1406/1986.

Boucher R. *Divan de Férazdak.* See Farazdaq, *Divan de Férazdak.*

Brag, M. F., and T. Thorelius. *Carmen Ashae. . . .* Lundæ 1842.

Brockelmann, Carl. *Geschichte der arabischen Litteratur.* 2 vols. Weimar 1898–1902. 3 Supplementbände, Leiden 1937–42.

al-Buḫārī, Muḥammad b. Ismācīl. *Ṣaḥīḥ,* with the *šarḥ* by al-Kirmānī. 24 vols. Cairo 1351–56/1932–38.

al-Buḥturī, al-Walīd b. cUbayd. *Dīwān Al-Boḥtorī.* Édition critique par Ḥasan Kāmil Aṣ-Ṣīrafī. 3rd ed., 5 vols. Cairo 1975.

———. *Le Kitâb al-Ḥamâsah de Abou cUbâdat al-Buḥturî.* Avec préface, tables, variantes et notes critiques par P. L. Cheikho. Beirut 1910.

———. *The Ḥamâsah of al-Buḥturî.* With Indexes by R. Geiger and D. S. Margoliouth. Leiden: E. J. Brill, 1909.

Cilardo, Agostino. *Diritto ereditario islamico delle scuole giuridiche ismailita e imamita: Casistica.* I.P.O.-I.U.O., Rome and Naples 1993.

———. *Diritto ereditario islamico delle scuole giuridiche sunnite (ḥanafita, mālikita, šāfiᶜita e ḥanbalita) e delle scuole giuridiche zaydita, ẓāhirita e ibāḍita: Casistica.* I.P.O.-I.U.O., Rome and Naples 1994.

———. "Preliminary Notes on the Qurʾānic Term *Kalāla.*" In *Law, Christianity and Modernism in Islamic Society: Proceedings of the Eighteenth Congress of the Union Européenne des Arabisants et Islamisants Held at the Katholieke Universiteit Leuven (September 3 – September 9, 1996).* Pp. 3-12. Louvain 1998.

———. *Studies on the Islamic Law of Inheritance.* In *AIUON.* Supplement no. 63 to vol. 50 (1990), fasc. 2. Naples 1990.

———. *Teorie sulle origini del diritto islamico.* I.P.O. Rome 1990.

Coulson, Noel. J. *Succession in the Muslim Family.* Cambridge 1971.

al-Ḏahabī, Muḥammad b. Aḥmad. *Kitāb Taḏkirat al-ḥuffāẓ.* 4 vols. Beirut 1375–77/1955–58.

al-Dāraquṭnī, ᶜAlī b. ᶜUmar. *Al-Sunan.* 4 vols. Medina 1386/1966.

al-Dārimī, ᶜAbd Allāh b. ᶜAbd al-Raḥmān. *Al-Musnad al-ǧāmiᶜ* or *al-Sunan.* 2 vols. Cairo 1386/1966.

Derenbourg, Hartwig. *Le Dîwân de Nâbiġa Dhobyânî.* Paris 1869.

Durant, Bernard. *Droit musulman: Droit successoral,* farâ'idh. Paris 1991.

Encyclopaedia of Islam (2d edition), Leiden 1960–.

Farazdaq. *Divan de Férazdak: récits de Mohammed-ben-Habib d'après Ibn-el-Arabi.* Publié sur le manuscrit de Sainte-Sophie de Constantinople, avec une traduction française par R. Boucher. Paris 1870.

———. *Dīwān al-Farazdaq.* 2 vols. Beirut 1380/1960.

al-Fattānī, ᶜAbd al-Malik b. ᶜAbd al-Wahhāb. *Ḫulāṣat al-Farāʾiḍ: naẓm al-Sirāǧiyya.* In *Kitāb Maǧmūᶜ min muhimmat al-mutūn.* Cairo 1328/1910.

First Encyclopaedia of Islam, 9 vols.; reprint, Leiden 1987.

al-Fīrūzābādī, Muḥammad b. Yaᶜqūb. *Al-Qāmūs al-muḥīṭ.* 4 vols. Būlāq 1301–3/1883–86; reprint, Beirut 1371/1952.

Furāt b. Ibrāhīm b. Furāt al-Kūfī. See Ibn Furāt al-Kūfī, Furāt.

al-Ǧawharī, Ismāᶜīl b. Ḥammād. *Kitāb Tāǧ al-luġa wa-ṣiḥāḥ al-ᶜarabiyya.* 2 vols. Būlāq 1282/1865.

Geyer, R. *Gedichte von 'Abû Baṣîr Maimûn Ibn Qays al-'A'šâ . . . und von Al-Musayyab Ibn 'Alas.* London 1928.

Goldfeld, Isaiah. "The *Tafsīr* of ᶜAbdallāh b. ᶜAbbās." *Der Islam* 58 (1981): 125–35.

Griffini, E. *"Corpus Juris"* di Zaid ibn ᶜAlī (VIII sec. Cr.). See Zayd b. ᶜAlī, *"Corpus Juris."*

al-Ǧubūrī, ᶜAbd Allāh Muḥammad. *Fiqh al-imām al-Awzāᶜī.* 2 vols. Baghdad 1397/1977.

Guidi, Ignazio. *Tables alphabétiques du Kitâb al-Aġânî.* 2 vols. Leiden 1895/1900.

Guillaume, A. *The Life of Muhammad.* See Ibn Hišām, *The Life of Muhammad.*

al-Ǧurǧānī, Abū ᵓl-ᶜAbbās Aḥmad b. Muḥammad. *Kitāb al-Kifāya fī maᶜrifat al-farāᵓiḍ wa-qismat al-mawārīṯ.* MS; cf. *GAL*, S, I, 505, no. 6.

Habīb b. Aws, Abū Tammām, al-Ṭāᵓī. *Dīwān.* Beirut 1887.

———. *Dīwān Abī Tammām (Poésie complète d'abi Tammam).* Avec l'explication d'al-Khaṭīb at-Tabrīzī. Édition critique par Moḥammad ᶜAbdo ᶜAzzām. 4 vols. Cairo 1976.

———. *Hamâsa, oder Die ältesten arabischen Volkslieder,* gesammelt von Abu Temmâm; übersetzt und erläutert von Fr. Rückert. 2 vols. Stuttgart 1846.

———. *Hamasae Carmina,* cum Tebrisii scholiis integris primum edidit, indicibus instruxit, versione Latina et commentario illustravit Georg. Guil. Freytag. 2 vols. Bonnæ 1828–51.

———. *L'index de la Ḥamasa d'Abou Tammam (Boulaq 1296) et des Moufaḍḍaliyat* (Caire 1324–1906). Arrangé d'après l'ordre alphabétique par O. Rescher. Stamboul 1914.

———. *The Díwán Hammásah,* A Selection of Arabic Poems by Aboo Tammám . . . Habíb Ibn Aws Al-Táyi, prepared . . . and edited by Mawlawi Kabír al-Dín Ahmad and Mawlawi Golam Rabbáni. Calcutta 1856.

al-Ḫalīl b. Aḥmad. *Kitāb al-ᶜAyn.* Ed. Mahdī al-Maḫzūmī and Ibrāhīm al-Sāmarrāᵓī. 8 vols. Beirut 1408/1988.

Ḫalīl b. Isḥāq. *Al-Muḫtaṣar.* Trans. I. Guidi and D. Santillana, *Il "Mukhtaṣar" o Sommario del diritto malechita.* 2 vols. Milan 1919.

Hallaq, Wael. B. *Law and Legal Theory in Classical and Medieval Islam.* Aldershot, UK, 1994.

Hell, Joseph. *Das Leben des Farazdaḳ nach seinen Gedichten und sein Loblied auf al-Walîd ibn Jazîd.* Leipzig 1903.

———. *Divan des Farazdak.* Photolith. Wiedergabe. 2 vols. Munich 1900.

———. Al-Farazdak̦'s Lieder auf die Muhallabiten." *ZDMG* 59 (1905): 589–621; 60 (1906): 1–48.

al-Ḥillī (al-ᶜAllāma). *Riǧāl al-ᶜAllāma al-Ḥillī.* See Ibn al-Muṭahhar al-Ḥillī, al-Ḥasan b. Yūsuf (al-ᶜAllāma), *Riǧāl al-ᶜAllāma al-Ḥillī.*

al-Ḥillī (al-Muḥaqqiq). *Šarāʾiᶜ al-Islām.* See al-Muḥaqqiq al-Ḥillī, Ǧaᶜfar b. al-Ḥasan, *Šarāʾiᶜ al-Islām.*

al-Ḫiraqī, ᶜUmar al-Ḥusayn. *Al-Muḫtaṣar.* In Ibn Qudāma, *al-Muġnī.*

Howell, Mortimer Sloper. *Grammar of the Classical Arabic Language . . . . of the Most Approved Native or Naturalized Authorities.* 7 vols. Allahabad 1880–1911.

al-Ḥumaydī, ᶜAbd Allāh b. al-Zubayr. *Al-Musnad.* Ed. Ḥabīb al-Raḥmān al-Aᶜẓamī. 2 vols. Karachi 1382/1963.

al-Ḫurāsānī al-Ibāḍī, Abū Ġānim Bišr b. Ġānim. *Al-Mudawwana al-kubrā.* Ed. Muḥammad b. Yūsuf Aṭfayyiš (LC: Aṭṭafayyish) al-Ibāḍī al-Ǧazāʾirī. Beirut 1394/1974.

Ibn Abī Ḥātim, ᶜAbd al-Raḥmān b. Muḥammad. *Kitāb al-Ǧarḥ waʾl-taᶜdīl.* 8 vols. Ḥaydarābād 1941–53.

Ibn Abī Šayba, ᶜAbd Allāh b. Muḥammad. *Al-Kitāb al-Muṣannaf fī ʾl-aḥādīṯ waʾl-āṯār.* Ed. ᶜAbd al-Ḫāliq al-Afġānī and ᶜĀmir al-ᶜUmrī al-Aᶜẓamī. 15 vols. Bombay 1399–1403/1979–83.

Ibn Abī Zayd al-Qayrawānī. *La Risâla ou Épitre sur les éléments du dogme et de la loi de l'Islam selon le rite mâlikite.* Texte arabe et traduction française avec un avant-propos, des notes et trois index par Léon Bercher. 5th ed. Alger 1960.

Ibn al-ᶜArabī, Muḥammad b. ᶜAbd Allāh. *Aḥkām al-Qurʾān.* Ed. Muḥammad ᶜAbd al-Qādir ᶜAṭā. 4 vols. Beirut 1408/1988.

Ibn al-Murtaḍā. Aḥmad b. Yaḥyā. *Kitāb al-Baḥr al-zaḫḫār al-ǧāmiᶜ li-maḏāhib ᶜulamāʾ al-amṣār.* 5 vols. Cairo 1366–68/1947–49.

Ibn al-Muṭahhar al-Ḥillī, al-Ḥasan b. Yūsuf (al-ᶜAllāma). *Riǧāl al-ᶜAllāma al-Ḥillī.* 2d ed. Al-Naǧaf 1381/1961.

Ibn al-Nadīm, Muḥammad b. Isḥāq. *Kitāb al-Fihrist.* Ed. Flügel. Leipzig 1871; ed. Cairo 1348/1929–30.

Ibn ᶜĀṣim, Muḥammad b. Muḥammad. *Traité de droit musulman: La Tohfat d'Ebn Acem.* Texte arabe avec traduction française, commentaire juridique & notes philologiques par O. Houdas et F. Martel, Alger 1882.

Ibn al-Aṯīr, Maǧd al-Dīn al-Mubārak b. Muḥammad. *Al-Nihāya fī ġarīb al-ḥadīṯ waʾl-aṯar.* On the margin: al-Suyūṭī, *al-Durr al-naṯīr: Talḫīṣ Nihāyat Ibn al-Aṯīr.* 4 vols. Cairo 1311/1893.

Ibn Bābawayh al-Qummī, Muḥammad b. ᶜAlī. *ᶜIlal al-šarāʾiᶜ.* Al-

Nağaf 1383/1963.

———. *Kitāb man lā yaḥḍuruhu ᵓl-faqīh.* 4 vols. Al-Nağaf 1377–78/1957–59.

———. *Maᶜānī al-aḫbār.* Al-Nağaf 1391/1971.

———. *Al-Muqniᶜ waᵓl-Hidāya.* Teheran 1377/1957–58.

———. *Musnad al-imām Riḍā.* 2 vols. Beirut 1403/1983.

Ibn Baraka, ᶜAbd Allāh b. Muḥammad. *Kitāb al-Ğāmiᶜ.* 2 vols. ᶜUmān 1983.

Ibn Durayd, Muḥammad b. al-Ḥasan. *Ğamharat al-luġa.* 4 vols. Baghdad n.d. (reprint of the Ḥaydarābād edition, 1344–51/1926–33).

Ibn Furāt al-Kūfī, Furāt. *Tafsīr Furāt al-Kūfī.* Ed. Muḥammad al-Kāẓim. 2 vols. Beirut 1412/1992.

Ibn Ḥağar al-ᶜAsqalānī, Aḥmad b. ᶜAlī. *Kitāb Tahḏīb al-Tahḏīb.* 12 vols. Ḥaydarābād 1325–27/1907–9; reprint, Beirut 1968.

Ibn Ḥanbal, Aḥmad b. Muḥammad. *Al-Musnad.* 6 vols. Cairo 1313/1895; reprint, Beirut 1405/1985.

Ibn Ḥazm, ᶜAlī b. Aḥmad. *Al-Iḥkām fī uṣūl al-aḥkām.* Ed. Aḥmad Muḥammad Šākir, 8 vols. Cairo n.d.

———. *Kitāb al-Muḥallā.* 11 vols. Beirut 1352/1969.

———. *Marātib al-iğmāᶜ fī ᵓl-ᶜibādāt waᵓl-muᶜāmalāt waᵓl-muᶜtaqadāt.* Beirut 1978.

Ibn Hišām, ᶜAbd al Malik. *Das Leben Muhammed's* nach Muhammed Ibn Ishâk, bearbeitet von Abd el-Malik Ibn Hischâm. Herausgegeben von F. Wüstenfeld. 3 vols. Göttingen 1858–60.

———. *Das Leben Mohammed's* nach Mohammed Ibn Ishak bearbeitet von Abd el-Malik Ibn Hischam. Aus dem Arabischen übersetzt von Gustav Weil, 2 vols., Stuttgart 1864.

———. *The Life of Muhammad.* A translation of Ibn Isḥāq's *Sīrat Rasūl Allāh* with introduction and notes by A. Guillaume. Oxford 1955.

Ibn Māğa, Muḥammad b. Yazīd. *Sunan.* 2 vols. Cairo 1372/ 1972.

Ibn Manẓūr, Muḥammad b. Mukarram. *Lisān al-ᶜArab.* 15 vols. Beirut 1374–76/1955–56.

Ibn Qays, Abū Isḥāq Ibrāhīm. *Muḫtaṣar al-Ḫiṣāl.* ᶜUmān 1403/1983.

Ibn Qudāma, Muwaffaq al-Dīn ᶜAbd Allāh b. Aḥmad. *Al-Kāfī fī fiqh al-imām Aḥmad b. Ḥanbal.* 3 vols. Damascus 1964.

———. *Al-Muġnī.* 12 vols. Cairo 1341–48/1922–30.

———. *Al-Muqniᶜ fī fiqh imām al-sunna Aḥmad b. Ḥanbal.* 2d ed. 3 vols. Cairo 1382/1962–63.

———. *Al-ᶜUmda fī fiqh imām al-sunna Aḥmad b. Ḥanbal al-Šaybānī.* Cairo 1385/1965–66.

Ibn Qutayba, ᶜAbd Allāh b. Muslim. *Liber poësis et poëtarum*, quem edidit M. J. De Goeje. Lugduni-Batavorum 1904.

Ibn Rašīq al-Qayrawānī, al-Ḥasan. *Al-ᶜUmda fī maḥāsin al-šiᶜr wa-ādābihi wa-naqdihi.* 2 vols. Cairo 1374/1955.

Ibn Saᶜd, Muḥammad. *Kitāb al-Ṭabaqāt al-kabīr.* Ed. E. Sachau. 9 vols. Leiden 1904–28.

———. *Kitāb al-Ṭabaqāt al-kubrā.* 8 vols. Beirut 1376–80/1957–60.

Ibn Sīda, ᶜAlī b. Ismāᶜīl. *Kitāb al-Muḥkam waʾl-muḥīṭ al-aᶜẓam fī ʾl-luġa.* Ed. Muṣṭafā al-Saqqā and Ḥusayn Naṣṣār. 7 vols. Cairo 1377–93/1958–73.

Ibn Wahb, ᶜAbd Allāh. *Le Djâmi' d'Ibn Wahb.* Édité et commenté par J. David-Weill. 2 vols. Cairo 1939–48.

Ibrāhīm b. Qays. *Muḫtaṣar al-Ḫiṣāl.* See Ibn Qays, Abū Isḥāq Ibrāhīm, *Muḫtaṣar al-Ḫiṣāl.*

Juynboll, G. H. A. *Muslim Tradition: Studies in Chronology, Provenance, and Authorship of the Early Ḥadīth.* Cambridge 1983.

———. "Nāfiᶜ, the *Mawlā* of Ibn ᶜUmar, and His Position in Muslim *Ḥadīth* Literature." *Der Islam* 70 (1993): 207–44.

al-Kaššī, Abū ᶜAmr Muḥammad b. ᶜUmar. *Riǧāl al-Kaššī.* Ed. Aḥmad al-Ḥusaynī. Bombay 1317/1899.

Khan, Mohammad Mustafa Ali. *Islamic Law of Inheritance: A New Approach.* New Delhi 1989.

al-Kindī, Aḥmad b. ᶜAbd Allāh. *Al-Muṣannaf.* Ed. ᶜAbd al-Munᶜim ᶜĀmir and Ǧād Allāh Aḥmad. 10 vols. Masqaṭ 1979–83.

al-Kulaynī, Muḥammad b. Yaᶜqūb. *Al-Uṣūl min al-Kāfī, al-Furūᶜ min al-Kāfī, al-Rawḍa min al-Kāfī.* Ed. ᶜAlī Akbar al-Ġaffārī. 8 vols. Tehran 1388–89/1967–68.

Lane, Edward. William. *An Arabic-English Lexicon.* 8 parts. New York 1955–56.

Lyall, Charles. *The Dīwāns of ᶜAbīd Ibn al-Abraṣ, of Asad, and ᶜĀmir Ibn aṭ-Ṭufail, of ᶜĀmir Ibn Ṣaᶜṣaᶜah.* Ed. for the first time . . . , and supplied with a translation and notes by Ch. Lyall. Leyden and London 1913.

———. *Translations of Ancient Arabian Poetry: Chiefly Pre-Islamic.* With an Introduction and Notes. London 1930.

Mālik b. Anas. *Kitāb al-Muwaṭṭaʾ.* Related by Yaḥyā b. Yaḥyā al-Layṯī al-Andalusī. With the *šarḥ* by Muḥammad b. ᶜAbd al-Bāqī b. Yūsuf al-Zurqānī. 4 vols. Cairo 1373/1954.

———. *Muwaṭṭā al-Imām Mālik.* Related by Muḥammad b. al-Ḥasan al-Šaybānī. With the *šarḥ* by ᶜAbd al-Ḥayy al-Laknawī. Ed. and cmt.

ᶜAbd al-Wahhāb ᶜAbd al-Laṭīf. 2d ed., Cairo 1387/1967.

———. *Al-Mudawwana al-kubrā, riwāyat al-Imām Saḥnūn b. Saᶜīd al-Tanūḫī.* 16 vols. Cairo 1323–24/1905.

al-Marwazī, Muḥammad b. Naṣr. *Al-Sunna.* Riyāḍ n.d.

Motzki, Harald. *Die Anfänge der islamischen Jurisprudenz: Ihre Entwicklung in Mekka bis zur Mitte des 2./8. Jahrhunderts.* Stuttgart 1991.

———. "Der Fiqh des -Zuhrī: die Quellenproblematik." *Der Islam* 68 (1991): 1–44.

———. "The *Muṣannaf* of ᶜAbd al-Razzāq al-Ṣanᶜānī as a Source of Authentic *Aḥādīth* of the First Century A.H." *Journal of Near Eastern Studies* 50/1 (1991): 1–21.

Muᶜallaqāt. English. *The Seven Golden Odes of Pagan Arabia: Known Also as the Moallakat.* Translated from the original Arabic by Anne Blunt; done into English verse by Wilfrid Scawen Blunt. London 1903.

Muḥammad ᶜAbduh and Muḥammad Rašīd Riḍā. *Tafsīr al-Qurʾān al-karīm*, known as *Tafsīr al-Manār.* 12 vols. Cairo 1372–73/1953–54.

Muḥammad al-Bāqir al-Bahbūdī. *Ṣaḥīḥ al-Kāfī.* See al-Bahbūdī, Muḥammad al-Bāqir, *Ṣaḥīḥ al-Kāfī.*

al-Muḥaqqiq al-Ḥillī, Ǧaᶜfar b. al-Ḥasan. *Recueil de lois concernant les musulmans schyites.* See Querry, Amédée, *Recueil de lois concernant les musulmans schyites.*

———. *Šarāʾiᶜ al-Islām fī masāʾil al-ḥalāl waʾl-ḥarām.* Ed. ᶜAbd al-Ḥusayn Muḥammad ᶜAlī. 4 vols. Al-Naǧaf 1389/1969.

al-Murtaḍā al-Zabīdī, Muḥammad b. Muḥammad. *Tāǧ al-ᶜarūs.* 10 vols. Cairo 1306–7/1888–90.

al-Muṣᶜabī, ᶜAbd al-ᶜAzīz b. Ibrāhīm. *Kitāb al-Nīl wa-šifāʾ al-ᶜalīl.* 2 vols. Cairo 1305/1887–88.

Muslim b. al-Ḥaǧǧāǧ al-Qušayrī. *Ṣaḥīḥ.* With the *šarḥ* by al-Nawawī. 18 vols. Cairo 1347–49/1929–30.

al-Mutanabbī, Abū ʾl-Ṭayyib. *Dīwān al-Mutanabbī.* Beirut 1377/1958.

al-Mutawakkil ᶜalā ʾllāh Aḥmad b. Sulaymān b. al-Hādī ilā ʾl-Ḥaqq, Caliph. *Kitāb Uṣūl al-aḥkām fī ʾl-ḥalāl waʾl-ḥarām.* MS; cf. *GAL*, S, I, 699.

al-Muzanī, Abū Ibrāhīm Ismāᶜīl b. Yaḥyā b. Ismāᶜīl. *Al-Muḫtaṣar.* On the margin of al-Šāfiᶜī, *Kitāb al-Umm.*

al-Nābiġa al-Ḏubyānī. *Dīwān al-Nābiġa al-Ḏubyānī.* Beirut 1379/1960.

———. See also Derenbourg, Hartwig.

al-Naǧāšī, Aḥmad b. ᶜAlī. *Kitāb al-Riǧāl*, or *Asmāʾ al-riǧāl.*

Bombay 1317/1899.

Nallino, Carlo Alfonso. *La littérature arabe des origines à l'époque de la dynastie umayyade.* Trad. franç. par Ch. Pellat, d'après la version it. de M. Nallino. Paris 1950 (*La letteratura araba* . . . , Rome 1948).

al-Nasafī, ᶜAbd Allāh b. Aḥmad. *Tafsīr al-Nasafī.* 4 vols. Cairo n.d.

al-Nawawī. *Minhâdj aṭ-Ṭâlibîn, Le guide des zélés croyants: Manuel de jurisprudence musulmane selon le rite de Châfi'î.* Texte arabe . . . avec traduction et annotations par L. W. C. van den Berg. 3 vols. Batavia 1882–84.

al-Nīsābūrī, Niẓām al-Dīn. *Tafsīr ġarāʾib al-Qurʾān wa-raġāʾib al-furqān.* On the margin of the *Tafsīr* of al-Ṭabarī. 30 vols. Cairo 1321/ 1903.

Nöldeke, Theodor. *Die Gedichte des 'Urwa ibn Alward.* Göttingen 1863.

al-Nuᶜmān b. Muḥammad, Abū Ḥanīfa. *Daᶜāʾim al-islām wa-ḏikr al-ḥalāl waʾl-ḥarām waʾl-qaḍāyā waʾl-aḥkām ᶜan ahl bayt rasūl Allāh.* Ed. Āṣif b. ᶜAlī Aṣġar Fayḍī. 2 vols. Cairo 1379–83/1960–63.

———. *Kitāb al-Iqtiṣār.* Ed. Muḥammad Waḥīd Mīrzā. Damascus 1376/1957.

———. *Minhāǧ al-farāʾiḍ.* MS; cf. *GAS*, I, 578, no. 22.

———. *Muḫtaṣar al-āṯār fī-mā ruwiya ᶜan al-aʾimma al-aṭhār.* MS; cf. GAS, I, 576, no. 1.

Powers, David Stephan. *Studies in Qur'an and* Ḥadīth: *The Formation of the Islamic Law of Inheritance.* Berkeley, Los Angeles and London 1986.

———. "The Islamic Law of Inheritance Reconsidered: A New Reading of Q. 4:12b." *Studia Islamica* 55 (1982): 61–94.

al-Qudūrī, Aḥmad b. Muḥammad. *Al-Muḫtaṣar.* Cairo 1367/1948.

Querry, Amédée. *Recueil de lois concernant les musulmans schyites.* (Trans. of the *Šarāʾiᶜ* by al-Muḥaqqiq al-Ḥillī.) 2 vols. Paris 1871–72.

al-Rāzī, Faḫr al-Dīn. *Mafātīḥ al-ġayb*, known as *al-Tafsīr al-kabīr.* 6 vols. Būlāq 1278/1862.

Russel, Alexander David, and ᶜAbdullah al-Maʾmūn Suhrawardy. *Muslim Law: An Historical Introduction to the Law of Inheritance.* London 1925.

Sachau, Eduard. "Muhammedanisches Erbrecht nach der Lehre der Ibaditischen Araber von Zanzibar und Ostafrika." In *Sitzungsberichte der K. Preussichen Akademie der Wissenschaften zu Berlin*, VIII, 1894. Italian trans. by I. Guidi, "Il diritto ereditario musulmano secondo la dottrina degli arabi ibaditi di Zanzibar e dell'Africa Orientale," in *Rivista Coloniale*, 1906, pp. 173–96, 335–87.

al-Šāfiᶜī, Muḥammad b. Idrīs. *Aḥkām al-Qurʾān.* (Collected by al-Bayhaqī.) 2 vols. Cairo 1371/1952.

———. *Kitāb al-Umm.* 7 vols. Cairo 1321–1325/1903–8.

———. *Kitāb Iḫtilāf al-ḥadīṯ.* On the margin of vol. VII of his *Kitāb al-Umm*

———. *Al-Risāla [al-qadīma].* In vol. VII of his Kitāb al-Umm.

———. *Al-Risāla [al-ǧadīda].* Ed. Aḥmad Muḥammad Šākir. Beirut 1358/1939.

———. *Tartīb Musnad al-Imām . . . al-Šāfiᶜī.* Ed. Muḥammad Zāhid b. al-Ḥasan al-Kawṯarī. 2 vols. Cairo 1369–70/1950–51.

Saḥnūn b. Saᶜīd al-Tanūḫī. *Al-Mudawwana al-kubrā.* See Mālik b. Anas, *al-Mudawwana al-kubrā.*

al-Saraḫsī, Muḥammad b. Aḥmad. *Kitāb al-Mabsūṭ.* 30 vols. Cairo 1324–31/1906–13.

———. *Šarḥ Kitāb al-Siyar al-kabīr.* In *Kitāb al-Siyar al-kabīr*, with the *šarḥ* by al-Saraḫsī. 4 vols. Ḥaydarābād 1335–36/1916–18.

al-Šaṭṭī, Muḥammad. *Risāla fī Masāʾil al-imām Dāwūd al-Ẓāhirī.* Damascus 1330/1912.

al-Ṣāwī, ᶜAbd Allāh Ismāᶜīl. *Šarḥ Dīwān al-Farazdaq.* Cairo 1354/ 1936.

al-Šaybānī, Muḥammad b. al-Ḥasan. *Al-Ǧāmiᶜ al-kabīr.* Ed. Abū ʾl-Wafāʾ al-Afġānī. Cairo 1356/ 1937.

———. *Al-Ḥuǧǧa fī iḫtilāf ahl al-Kūfa wa-ahl al-Madīna.* MS; cf. *GAL*, I, 180, no. XI; S, I, 291, no. XI; *GAS*, I, 432, no. XII.

———. *Kitāb al-Siyar al-kabīr.* Cf. al-Saraḫsī, *Šarḥ Kitāb al-Siyar al-kabīr.*

Schacht, Joseph. *The Origins of Muhammadan Jurisprudence.* Oxford 1950.

Schwarz, P. "Al-Farazdaḳ's Lieder auf die Muhallabiten: Eine Nachlese." *ZDMG* 73 (1919): 80–126.

Sezgin, Fuat. *Geschichte des arabischen Schrifttums.* 9 vols. Leiden 1967–84.

al-Subkī, Taqī al-Dīn b. ᶜAbd al-Kāfī. *Fatāwā al-Subkī.* 2 vols. Cairo 1356/1965.

Sufyān b. Saᶜīd al-Ṯawrī. "Frühislamisches Erbrecht nach dem *Kitāb al-Farāʾiḍ* des Sufyān al-Thawrī." Edition und Kommentar von Hans-Peter Raddatz. *Die Welt des Islams* 13 (1971): 26–78.

———. *Tafsīr al-Qurʾān al-karīm.* Ed. Imtiyāz ᶜAlī ᶜAršī. Rāmpūr 1385/1965.

al-Suyūṭī. *Al-Durr al-naṯīr.* See Ibn al-Aṯīr, *al-Nihāya fī ġarīb al-ḥadīṯ wa'l-aṯar.*

———. *Kitāb Isʿāf al-mubaṭṭa' bi-riǧāl al-Muwaṭṭa'.* (Following his copy of *al-Muwaṭṭa'* by Mālik.) 2 vols. Cairo 1370/1951.

———. *Ṭabaqāt al-ḥuffāẓ.* Ed. ʿAlī Muḥammad ʿUmar. Cairo 1393/1973.

al-Ṭabarī. *Ǧāmiʿ al-Bayān ʿan al-Qur'ān: Tafsīr al-Ṭabarī.* Ed. Maḥmūd Muḥammad Šākir and Aḥmad Muḥammad Šākir. 16 vols. Cairo 1374–89/1954–69.

al-Ṭabarsī, al-Faḍl b. al-Ḥasan. *Maǧmaʿ al-Bayān fī Tafsīr al-Qur'ān.* 6 vols. Beirut 1957.

al-Ṭaḥāwī, Aḥmad b. Muḥammad. *Iḫtilāf al-fuqahā'.* Ed. Muḥammad Ṣaġīr Ḥasan al-Maʿṣūmī. Islāmābād 1391/1971.

———. *Al-Muḫtaṣar.* Ed. Abū 'l-Wafā' al-Afġānī. Cairo 1370/1950.

al-Ṭayālisī, Abū Dāwūd Sulaymān b. Dāwūd. *Kitāb al-Musnad.* Ḥaydarābād 1321/ 1903.

Thorbecke, H. "Al-Aʿšâ's Lobgedichte auf Muḥammad." In *Morgenländische Forschungen:* Festschrift H. L. Fleischer zu seinem funfzigjährigen Doctorjubiläum am. 4. März 1874, gewidmet von seinen Schülern H. Derenbourg . . . [et al.], pp. 233–60. Leipzig 1875.

al-Tibrīzī, Yaḥyā b. ʿAlī. *A Commentary on Ten Ancient Arabic Poems.* Ed. Charles James Lyall, Calcutta 1894; 2d ed., 1965.

al-Tirmiḏī, Muḥammad b. ʿĪsā. *Kitāb al-Sunan* or *al-Ǧāmiʿ al-ṣaḥīḥ.* 5 vols. Cairo 1384–87/1965–67.

al-Ṭūsī, Muḥammad b. al-Ḥasan. *Al-Fihrist* or *Fihrist kutub al-Šīʿa.* Ed. Muḥammad Ṣādiq Āl Baḥr al-ʿUlūm. 2d ed. Al-Naǧaf 1380/1960.

———. *Al-Istibṣār fī-mā iḫtalafa min al-aḫbār.* Ed. Ḥasan al-Mūsawī. al-Ḫarsān. 2d ed. 4 vols. Al-Naǧaf 1376/1957.

———. *Kitāb al-Ḫilāf.* 3 vols. Al-Naǧaf 1956.

———. *Riǧāl al-Ṭūsī.* Ed. Muḥammad Ṣādiq Āl Baḥr al-ʿUlūm. Al-Naǧaf 1381/1961.

———. *Tahḏīb al-Aḥkām.* 10 vols. Al-Naǧaf 1377–82/1957–62.

———. *Al-Tibyān fī tafsīr al-Qur'ān.* Ed. Āġā Buzurq al-Ṭihrānī and others. 10 vols. Al-Naǧaf 1376–83/1957–63.

Ullmann, Manfred. *Wörterbuch der klassischen arabischen Sprache.* Band I. Wiesbaden 1970.

Weil, Gustav. *Die poetische Literatur der Araber vor und unmittelbar nach Mohammed: Eine historisch-kritische Skizze.* Stuttgart and Tübingen 1837.

Wensinck, A. J. (Arent Jan). *Concordance et indices de la tradition musulmane.* 7 vols. Leiden 1936–69.

Yāqūt b. ʿAbd Allāh al-Hamawī. *Iršād al-arīb ilā maʿrifat al-adīb.* Ed. D. S. Margoliouth. 7 vols. London 1923–31.

al-Zabīdī. *Tāǧ al-ʿarūs.* See al-Murtaḍā al-Zabīdī, *Tāǧ al-ʿarūs.*

Zayd b. ʿAlī. *"Corpus Juris."* Ed. Eugenio Griffini. Milan 1919.

al-Ziriklī, Ḫayr al-Dīn. *Al-Aʿlām.* 2d ed. 10 vols. Cairo 1373–78/1954–59.

INDEX

JAIS MONOGRAPHS
SERIES EDITOR: JOSEPH NORMENT BELL

The *JAIS Monographs* series accompanies the *Journal of Arabic and Islamic Studies*, published by Edinburgh University Press.

The *Journal* seeks to promote the study of Arabic language and linguistics, medieval and modern Arabic literature, and Islamic civilisation through the dissemination of peer-reviewed research articles and review articles. Contributions published by the *Journal* are as a rule based primarily on materials in Arabic and other Near Eastern languages. Research based on sources in Western languages is also published in instances where the editors consider the material especially relevant to the purposes of the *Journal*.

Jacket image: an illuminated page from a Qur'ān, Egypt, c. 1300, ink, color, gold on paper. Reproduced with permission of H. P. Kraus, Inc., New York.

Jacket design concept: River Design, Edinburgh

Edinburgh University Press
22 George Square
Edinburgh EH8 9LF

www.eup.ed.ac.uk

ISBN 0 7486 1916 X

EU Authorised Representative:
Easy Access System Europe Mustamäe tee 50, 10621 Tallinn, Estonia
gpsr.requests@easproject.com

Printed and bound by CPI Group (UK) Ltd, Croydon, CR0 4YY
17/06/2026
02141225-0001